Teach®
Yourself

Sweet and Simple Knitting Projects

Sally Walton

For UK order enquiries: please contact Bookpoint Ltd,
130 Milton Park, Abingdon, Oxon OX14 4SB.
Telephone: +44 (0) 1235 827720. Fax: +44 (0) 1235 400454.
Lines are open 09.00–17.00, Monday to Saturday, with a 24-hour
message answering service. Details about our titles and how to
order are available at www.teachyourself.com

For USA order enquiries: please contact McGraw-Hill Customer
Services, PO Box 545, Blacklick, OH 43004-0545, USA.
Telephone: 1-800-722-4726. Fax: 1-614-755-5645.

For Canada order enquiries: please contact McGraw-Hill
Ryerson Ltd, 300 Water St, Whitby, Ontario L1N 9B6, Canada.
Telephone: 905 430 5000. Fax: 905 430 5020.

Long renowned as the authoritative source for self-guided
learning – with more than 50 million copies sold worldwide –
the **Teach Yourself** series includes over 500 titles in the fields
of languages, crafts, hobbies, business, computing and education.

British Library Cataloguing in Publication Data: a catalogue record
for this title is available from the British Library.

Library of Congress Catalog Card Number: on file.

First published in UK 2006 by Hodder Education, part of
Hachette Livre UK, 338 Euston Road, London, NW1 3BH.

First published in US 2006 by The McGraw-Hill Companies, Inc.

This edition published 2010.

Previously published as *Teach Yourself Knitting*

The **Teach Yourself** name is a registered trade mark of
Hodder Headline.

Typeset by MPS Limited, a Macmillan Company.

Printed in Great Britain for Hodder Education, an Hachette UK
Company, 338 Euston Road, London NW1 3BH, by CPI Cox &
Wyman, Reading, Berkshire RG1 8EX.

The publisher has used its best endeavours to ensure that the URLs
for external websites referred to in this book are correct and active
at the time of going to press. However, the publisher and the
author have no responsibility for the websites and can make no
guarantee that a site will remain live or that the content will remain
relevant, decent or appropriate.

Hachette UK's policy is to use papers that are natural, renewable
and recyclable products and made from wood grown in sustainable
forests. The logging and manufacturing processes are expected to
conform to the environmental regulations of the country of origin.

Impression number   10 9 8 7 6 5 4 3 2 1

Year   2014 2013 2012 2011 2010

Acknowledgements

A very big thank you to the knitters who helped me with this book: Jane Scruton, Tisha Dunn, Jilly Sillem, Lois Waldron, Debra Cocks and Elaine Hayes.

Thanks also to the good people at Rowan Yarns, Sirdar and Twilleys of Stamford for supplying yarns and equipment for the photographs.

And thanks to Michelle Garrett for her beautiful photographs and to her assistant, Lisa, for her technical wizardry.

Gratitude to my family for putting up with my continuing obsession with knitting.

Image credits

Front cover: © Andy Crawford/Dorling Kindersley/Getty Images

Back cover: © Jakub Semeniuk/iStockphoto.com, © Royalty-Free/Corbis, © agencyby/iStockphoto.com, © Andy Cook/iStockphoto.com, © Christopher Ewing/iStockphoto.com, © zebicho – Fotolia.com, © Geoffrey Holman/iStockphoto.com, © Photodisc/Getty Images, © James C. Pruitt/iStockphoto.com, © Mohamed Saber – Fotolia.com

Contents

Meet the author

My life-long love affair began at seven when I learned French knitting at school. In no time at all I was turning out bright knitted cords, swapping different coloured wool with friends and comparing techniques and results. Many years have passed and I now knit with two needles, not a cotton reel, but I am still sharing patterns, exchanging wool and enjoying the sociability of knitting with friends.

Initially there seems a lot remember – to hold the needles just so, twist the wool around your fingers, feed it through, pull it tight – but not too tight. Persevere. Once you have grasped the basics they stay with you forever.

My advice is to take it slowly. All these actions will quickly become automatic and you will soon progress to reading patterns and actually making things.

I confess that I struggled to read knitting patterns until I realized that there is no mysterious code to break – abbreviations are simply space-savers and without them patterns would all be way too long. You soon remember those you use regularly, and the others can be looked up whenever you need them.

Some knitters achieve the greatest satisfaction from being able to reproduce a pattern exactly, while others prefer to interpret patterns and add their own touches of individuality. I like to do a bit of both, depending on my mood.

My hope is that this book will not only teach you how to knit, but to love knitting and keep on knitting for the rest of your life.

Sally Walton

Only got a minute?

One of the best things about knitting is that you need very little skill or knowledge to get started. All you need is a ball of yarn and two needles, and most of us can learn to knit in a single session.

Knitting is a great takeaway hobby – you can knit wherever you go, apart from on planes where your needles are seen as lethal weapons!

Needle sizes refer to their width. They are shown either in US, European or English sizes, which can be confusing, so a needle gauge is a useful tool to have – it has different-sized holes that you can slide a needle through to check its size, whatever country you happen to be in.

Needles also come in different lengths, but only the width affects the way the stitches look. The length decides how many stitches fit on the needle and how wide your knitting will be.

Short needles are best for teaching children to knit – and also better on public transport where longer ones may irritate the person sitting next to you.

The most basic stitch is called 'knit' or 'plain', and the pattern that rows of this stitch make is called 'garter stitch'. It is the doggy paddle of knitting – it's where we all begin.

Garter stitch stretches in both directions, and is ideal for baby clothes and scarves.

The second stitch to learn is 'purl'. This is knitted after a plain row to make 'stocking stitch', which is the classic shop-bought knitted garment stitch. These two stitches will see you through a lifetime of knitting.

Knitters are a generally a friendly bunch and, because it's not competitive, advice is freely given (for example, 'Left-handers can learn stitches by looking at the diagrams in a mirror.'). It is also a great age leveller.

One of the most common things you will say as a knitter is, 'When I get to the end of this row…'.

5 Only got five minutes?

Be warned – knitting can be compulsive, especially when the bug first bites. It's a bit like falling in love: at first you can't get enough, but eventually you settle down into a less frantic relationship. It is a skill once learned never forgotten, like riding a bicycle.

The quickest way to learn is for someone to stand behind you, holding your hands and the needles, and take you through the movements. Lots of us learned this way, sitting on our mother's knee. If you are too big to sit on a knee, ask a patient knitter to sit beside you as you learn and guide you through what your hands need to do. Once you know how to knit, these movements become automatic.

Holding the needles correctly from the word go will help to develop your knitting rhythm, and this is what gives your work a nice even texture. Diagrams are very useful for reminding you of your hand and yarn positions when making the stitches.

Everyone learns differently and if you like instant results, learn simple garter stitch and make a scarf. The sense of achievement will drive you on until you tire of garter stitch, when you can progress to purl and knit stocking stitch.

Never stop knitting halfway along the row – it is a recipe for dropped stitches. A dropped stitch makes a hole that will run down through the rows below like a ladder in tights. If you do drop a stitch, don't panic, it can be picked up and worked back up the 'run' using a crochet hook.

Knitting is a sociable activity that involves long stretches when you can knit, talk, laugh and listen, interspersed with occasional moments of deep concentration. Even people who find it hard to walk and talk at the same time seem able to chat and knit.

The arrival of a new baby often triggers a desire to knit. This is perfectly natural, and the great thing about knitting for babies is that they are very small. Their little hats, socks and jumpers are relatively quick to knit, and these gifts will be all the more special and loved for being handmade.

Knitting yarns have come a long way since the days of itchy wools and garish nylons, and the choice available now is breathtaking. You can buy machine washable wool, British alpaca and organic cotton, silk, bamboo and even yarns spun from milk. There are yarns to appeal to environmentalists, vegans and knitters who would prefer to know that their yarn has been ethically sourced and produced. Colours change with the seasons and textures change with fashion.

The recognized term to describe all your yarn that is waiting to be knitted is 'your stash'!

Knitting can be both a verb and a noun, so you can say 'I am knitting' while you do it, then 'look at my fabulous knitting' when it's done.

10 Only got ten minutes?

Knitting is a craft with none of the usual barriers. You can take it up at any age and progress from learning the basics to confidently going it alone in hours rather than days, weeks or years. If you have a day to spare you will be able to call yourself a knitter by the end of it.

Knitting is a productive way to fill those 'wasted' hours spent waiting for and travelling on buses and trains or watching television. Believe me, once you have been bitten by the knitting bug you'll see any hands-free activity as a hands-on opportunity. If you are doing something that doesn't require holding on, you may just be able to knit at the same time, although in some cases there may be safety issues!

Knitting can be done on the cheap too, so affordability is not an issue. A ball of yarn and a set of needles are all you need to get started and, if you are on a tight budget, it is worth looking for these in charity shops. These are also a good source of vintage patterns and buttons and, as the wheel of fashion keeps turning around, you may just find this year's latest look lurking in a pile of old patterns.

Mention knitting to your friends and you will be surprised how many already have the skill and will be happy to be given a reason to get their own needles out and show you how it is done. Anyone who has let their knitting lapse will soon be inspired to start again when they see the fabulous new yarns that are on sale. Once upon a time the choice was between wool or nylon. How things have changed since crafts became cool! The colour ranges, textures and sheer variety of yarns are quite overwhelming – in a good way.

One consequence of the knitting revival is that new yarn shops are opening all the time, and they have evolved into much more than a place to buy yarn – they are knitting destinations – places to pass the time of day, take classes, make friends, hang out and be inspired. Check your local directory or look online at www.knitmap.com, a worldwide directory of local knitting shops, because you never know – your yarn heaven may be just around the corner.

I have yet to come across a person who wanted to learn to knit and failed. You will feel all fingers and thumbs to begin with, but that's always the case when you try something new.

It is definitely much easier to learn on a piece of knitting that is already a few rows underway. Persuade someone to help you get started by casting on ten to twenty stitches and slowly knitting about five rows plus a few stitches into the following row. Watch closely as they knit – ask questions, then take over. Having something 'joined-up' to hold on to will make it so much easier. You will also be able to see what should be happening when you insert the needle, wrap the wool and drop the stitch off.

If you don't have a knitting friend, do not despair – it is perfectly possible to learn on your own. A little struggle is no bad thing because you will have an even greater sense of achievement if you teach yourself.

A scarf is the perfect project to start with, and the most neck-hugging stretchy scarves are knitted in garter stitch. This is basic knitting, the first stitch you learn and my all-time favourite. One of its greatest charms is that it never looks quite as nice when mass-produced by machine as it does when knitted by hand.

When you first start knitting it is tempting to opt for thick yarn knitted on big needles. On the plus side, this is fun because you feel proportionately child-sized again and your knitting grows rewardingly fast. A word of warning though: you may find you get into bad habits because the way you hold the yarn and needles influences the rhythm of your knitting, which in turn affects its texture.

It is better to learn on mid-sized needles with double knitting (DK) or Arran yarn then, once you've got the hang of it, you can experiment.

Knitting soon becomes automatic – your hands remember what they have to do and they get on with it. This is what makes knitting with friends so enjoyable. You can carry on all your usual conversations with the odd interruption for stitch and row counting or serious concentration on tricky bits. Knitting has a way of ironing out age barriers and social differences between people too – it is a great leveller.

The online knitting community grows bigger every day. It began with knitters blogging, showing off their creations and receiving feedback and pictures from other knitters. It soon became obvious that the internet was a perfect place for knitters to make friends with each other and exchange ideas, patterns and problems. The blogs became clubs that started online yarn shops, and business is booming. The nice thing is that you can be a part of a discussion, post pictures of your projects or chat online with members on the other side of the world without spending any money. Knitters are generous with their time, knowledge and goodwill.

A knitting group can be a lot of fun, giving old friends a reason to meet regularly and introducing new people who might not meet otherwise. A city can be as lonely as the remotest place in the country and a knitting group can be a real social lifeline. There are groups meeting in wine bars, village halls, tea rooms, yarn stores and each other's homes all over the country, and if you can't find one perhaps you could start one.

Remember that most of us don't knit because we need something made out of yarn; we do it because we love knitting and the results are a bonus. If you can't think of a project, remember that charities always need knitted donations, and whether it is a vest for a newborn baby, a rug for a dog or a square for a patchwork blanket, this is another way that knitting can connect us and make our world seem a better, smaller and friendlier place.

1

Introduction

History of knitting

Amazing but true – there was life on earth before knitting! It is impossible to tell who had the idea first, but we can assume that it was nomadic tribes who herded animals and spun yarn from their fleeces. Everyday knitted garments would have been worn until they fell apart, so all ancient fragments that remain are those of fine ceremonial relics and we can only guess the real history of domestic knitting.

There is evidence to suggest that knitting originated in Arab countries, as knitted items have been found in Egyptian burial chambers. In fact, the discovery of an unusual sock divided at the big toe seems to prove that Englishmen were not the first to wear socks with sandals! Peruvians were spinning llama and alpaca knitting wool and dying it brilliant colours long before Europeans arrived to 'civilize' the South American continent. Some of the earliest knitting of all was a type of fringing made for the edges of woven cloth in pre-Columbian Peru. The Nazca tribes who lived there thousands of years ago developed a pattern style that involved many bright colour changes to depict human and animal forms.

A knitting Madonna is featured in a 15th-century Italian painting, which suggests that knitting was a familiar Renaissance pastime, and knitting guilds were set up during the Middle Ages in England to produce and trade in high-quality knitted garments. These guilds were made up of groups of highly skilled male knitters, and the only women ever allowed to join were the widows of members who had died.

The invention of the knitting frame, and, later, a machine capable of producing hundreds of pairs of identically perfect stockings, signalled the decline of hand knitting, although it remained popular in isolated communities.

Women knitted in a different style, using a knitting sheath or stick at the waist to hold one of the needles rigidly next to the body. A decorative carved sheath was a favourite courtship present given by a young man to his sweetheart. Knitting patterns were not written down but taught and handed down from mother to daughter, often as closely guarded family secrets. When fishermen sailed to other ports, patterns were exchanged or surreptitiously copied by local knitters. It has been only relatively recently that the value of these folk arts and crafts has been appreciated by a wider audience than the communities who traditionally practised them. Folklore tells of each fishing port having its own pattern so that a drowned sailor could be identified and returned to his home for burial.

The Aran Islands that lie off the west coast of Ireland have given their name to a unique knitting style made up of intricately interwoven Celtic cable patterns. They take inspiration from ancient Celtic symbols and the ropes and chains of fishing boats. Aran wool has traditionally been spun from the fleeces of the local sheep, which survive the most inhospitable climate and bleak landscape by living on a diet of seaweed dragged ashore by the fishermen. Traditionally, Aran fishermen's sweaters were knitted in the undyed creamy white wool that was rich in oily lanolin, using patterns designed to maximize its insulating properties. Aran wool is now dyed in a broad range of colours, and Aran is still one of the most popular and challenging knitting styles because of the variety of different stitches used for each garment.

The Shetland Islands lie off the north coast of Scotland. The islanders have a tradition of knitting square, fine lace shawls inspired by fine

Spanish lace brought to the islands in the 16th century. It seems that the women of the Shetland Islands developed the particular skill of weaving especially fine yarns and would knit shawls five feet square that were fine enough to be pulled through a wedding ring. The wool was also exceptionally soft because the island sheep shed their fleeces naturally in the summer and could be plucked rather than shorn. This produced long strands with tapering ends. The knitted shawl patterns have an intricate look but are constructed from a combination of relatively simple stitches. The completed shawls are washed and pegged out on a frame to dry naturally, which 'sets' their square shape.

The colourful and patterned Fairisle knitting takes its name from another small Shetland island. Legend tells that a galleon from the Spanish Armada was wrecked off Fair Isle in the 16th century and sailors were washed up onto the shore wearing brilliantly coloured patterned knitted garments. Imagine the mixed emotions on the shore with the pity for the poor drowned sailor being overwhelmed by excitement over his fabulous jumper!

The islanders copied and reinterpreted the patterns, and the name Fairisle is still synonymous with the knitting style. It is traditionally knitted in the round on four needles so that the right side is always facing outwards and only plain knit stitch is used on small areas of colour. The wool is simply carried across the back of the work and picked up again when needed. Originally, they dyed wool in muted shades using homemade vegetable dyes, but when synthetic dyes became available in the early 20th century the patterns took on a new vibrancy. The islanders presented the then Duke of Windsor with a knitted sweater when he visited them in the 1920s, and this unwitting product placement launched a Fairisle fashion when he was photographed wearing it to play a round of golf in the south of France. He is also credited with popularizing the Argyle sock pattern, a knitted tartan made using a technique called intarsia to knit blocks of colour.

The 'gansey' sweater, knitted for and by the fishermen of Guernsey, is the prototype for most of the fisherman's sweaters – or jerseys – whose name is derived from a different Channel island. They were knitted from dark blue dyed local wool that had a similar thickness to our double knitting but worked on much finer needles than we would use today. Sets of double-pointed needles or wires were used to knit the main body in the round, creating a tight water- and wind-repelling fabric. The women of Guernsey are known to have formed knitting cooperatives and traded to other fishing communities as long ago as the 16th century. Similar sweater styles existed in Cornwall and around the coast of Scotland.

There is an ancient tradition of knitting in Sweden, Norway and Finland, where the winters are extremely cold and communities can be snowed in for many months of the year. The Scandinavians contrasted their snow-white landscape with highly decorative homes, and their everyday garments show their skill and love of pattern. They used distinctive motifs and often worked in starkly contrasting black and white. Dates and initials are often incorporated, either knitted in or embroidered onto the knitted mittens, stockings and caps. Patterns such as reindeer, rose petals, people and chequer boards were the most popular in Norway.

Cable stitching was another popular feature, and fitted cardigans were made with geometrical bands of pattern around the neck, yolk and sleeves.

In Tunisia, shepherds have always knitted while tending their flocks. The product of their labours is the traditional red fez, which is knitted as a long tube then boiled up to make felt that is shaped on a block. Just like that!

Women famously knitted socks and Balaclavas to send to soldiers fighting in the First and Second World Wars. It meant far more to the soldiers than merely a way of keeping warm, as the knitting had been done by the soft hands of a woman back home. The knitting nurtured them and lifted their spirits. And, for the women, it provided a way to contribute and participate in the war effort even though they were far away from the Front.

In the 1950s and 1960s fashion favoured the new synthetic fabrics and home knitting fell from grace for a while. Then 'Earth Mothers' in fringed shawls knitted patchwork blankets to keep the hippies warm in the early 1970s, and Fairlisle tank tops came back into vogue as the thing for a young man to be seen in when strutting his stuff in bellbottoms and a fitted velvet jacket. The last 'big' knitting revival was in the 1980s when huge batwing, padded-shouldered mohair creations were a fashion essential, along with very spiky hair and tight leggings. Motif knitting was all the rage, too, with anything from teddies to tigers adorning sweaters worn by young and old alike. The nature of fashion is that it changes, and hand knitting kept a low profile during the minimalist nineties.

Knitting has staged a 21st-century comeback as a high-style craft activity. It's a worldwide phenomenon – championed by everyone from the anti-capitalist youth culture that venerates all things local, ethical and small scale to models and film stars with money to buy anything their heart desires but a craving for the down-to-earth rarity of handmade fashion. Theories as to the origins of knitting's new wave of popularity abound, but, in the end, knitting is something that you cannot pretend to do. You either knit and enjoy it or you don't, and no amount of paparazzi pictures of rock chicks knitting will make a knitter out of a quitter.

Hand-knitted clothes and home accessories have added value because they involve knitting for pleasure. We don't make sweaters, hats, gloves, warmers and throws from necessity anymore, as these things are mostly cheaper to buy ready made. Cheaper perhaps, but not unique. We knit for the love of it and to make something ourselves to keep or to be given away with our love.

The rhythmic, repetitive activity of knitting has a calming effect and combats stress in the same way as yoga or meditation does, but with knitting we get something afterwards that we can hold in our hands.

Learning to knit gives us a chance to express our creative selves in colour and texture and, what's more, to do it more or less anywhere, anytime – while having a conversation, sunbathing, watching TV or travelling on a train.

There are new knitting groups starting up all over the world, meeting on arranged 'knit nights' in cafés, bars and one another's homes to spend time together sharing their projects and stitches. Tap 'knitting' into any internet search engine and you will find a wealth of free patterns, advice, anecdotes and friendship. Knitters like to share.

Let's face it: knitting is pretty cool in the 21st century.

The downside is that it can be ever so slightly addictive.

Knitting equipment

All you need in order to learn to knit is a ball of yarn and a pair of straight needles. The size of the needles and the weight of the wool you choose for your first attempt will make a big difference to both experience and results. Knitting needles come in a range of sizes from very fine 2 mm that are used to knit fine lacy shawls, to the very fat virtual broomsticks for super chunky yarns.

Ideally, when you begin you need to use needles that are small enough to hold correctly and comfortably; 4–5 mm are ideal. When you start off holding the needles in the correct position, your knitting style is destined to develop into an effortlessly smooth rhythm. I would recommend using a medium-weight yarn, such as double knitting, to begin with. Your garment will take a while longer to grow than with chunky yarn, but knitting is as much about enjoying the activity as seeing the results.

Learn on big needles using chunky yarn and you will have to clutch the needles in your fists and lift your whole arm to move the yarn between the needles, making you feel like a toddler. The upside is that fat needles and chunky yarns give quick results. If you are impatient or desperately need that scarf then this route will suit you best.

KNITTING NEEDLES

Choose needles made from plastic, aluminium, wood, bamboo or a milk protein called casein. We all prefer one sort to another and you need to knit with them to make up your mind. Needles are sold in a range of different sizes and lengths.

Plastic needles
These are lightweight and slightly bendy.

Buy high-quality named brands because cheaper needles have too much 'give' in them.

The small plastic needles do not suit heavyweight garments but the larger-sized needles are tubular and very strong.

They come in a range of bright colours – especially the vintage needles that can be picked up cheaply second hand. On the downside, the old ones were made of a more brittle material that can snap under pressure.

Aluminium needles
Aluminium is a very light, strong metal – ideal for making knitting needles. These needles will last a lifetime and make a pleasant clicking noise when you knit. Stitches slip off easily, sometimes too easily, resulting in dropped stitches.

Old needles were made in a beautiful range of metallic colours, but nowadays they tend to be coated with grey enamel. The neutral grey background has obviously been proved to give stitches most definition when knitting and counting.

Bamboo needles

Polished bamboo needles are very popular with experienced knitters. It's a lightweight, strong and natural material that is a pleasure to hold in your hands. The only downside is that being made from a natural fibrous material the needles do occasionally have irregularities that cause them to split or splinter. When this happens they will shred the yarn. Spend a little extra to ensure high quality.

Insight

New sets can be expensive and needles don't wear out – help save the planet by buying second-hand needles. Hand-me-down needles may not be sized as metric. The English low numbers are large and the fine ones reach double figures. For example: metric 3 mm = English 11.

Cable needles

These are very short needles, sometimes with a dip in the middle, called a crank. They are used for knitting cable patterns. They come in a range of sizes to match the thickness of the knitting needles.

Circular needles

A circular needle is two short needles joined by a length of nylon or plastic. They are made in the standard range of needle sizes, and the length of the flexible section also varies to allow for different-sized tubes to be knitted. They can also be used conventionally when knitting large items like blankets, as the main weight of the knitting can lie in your lap instead of being carried on the needles.

Insight

If the connecting nylon keeps twisting back into its packaged shape, try warming it in hot water for a few minutes. Pull it straight between the needles and when it cools it will stay that way.

Double-pointed needles

These are used in sets of four or five to knit tubular items such as socks. They are also used for Fairisle knitting patterns.

Knitting needles conversion chart			
	Continental (mm)	English	US
	$2\frac{1}{4}$	13	0
	$2\frac{3}{4}$	12	1
	3	11	2
	$3\frac{1}{4}$	10	3
	$3\frac{3}{4}$	9	4
	4	8	5
	$4\frac{1}{2}$	7	6
	5	6	7
	$5\frac{1}{2}$	5	8
	6	4	9
	$6\frac{1}{2}$	3	10
	7	2	$10\frac{1}{2}$
	$7\frac{1}{2}$	1	11
	$8\frac{1}{2}$	00	13
	9	000	15

NEEDLE GAUGE

Knitting needles used to be numbered differently in the UK from the rest of Europe, but new needles are now all metric. The USA has a different system. Refer to the chart for the full range.

A gauge is invaluable for checking the sizes of odd, old or foreign needles.

STITCH HOLDERS

These are made in a range of sizes and are used to hold stitches that are not being knitted. When garments divide for a neckline, for instance, one half of the stitches are knitted while the other must wait their turn on a stitch holder.

Small numbers of stitches – such as the thumb of a glove – can be kept on safety pins, but care should be taken as they can catch and shred the yarn.

SEWING NEEDLES

A wool supplier will have specialist needles for making up knitted garments. A tapestry needle or a darning needle can also be used. Choose one with a rounded end rather than a sharp point that can shred yarns.

Insight

OUCH! Keep a small zip-up purse in your knitting bag for 'sharps' like scissors, a darning needle and some pins.

MEASURING EQUIPMENT

A rule
A rigid clear plastic rule is the best tool for checking tension squares.

> ### Insight
> It is always advisable to knit a tension square of 10 cm × 10 cm before you start work on a pattern. This will ensure that your knitting will be the right size for the number of stitches. See pages 135–136 for guidance on knitting a tension square.

Tape measure
A small retractable tape measure is ideal for measuring your knitting.

> ### Insight
> US measurements are non-metric. Be sure to convert ALL inches to centimetres before you begin to knit a US pattern, as this will prevent confusion and disasters later on.

PINS

Bright plastic-headed stainless steel pins are used when blocking and pressing garments before making up.

SCISSORS

You will need a small pair of blunt-ended scissors to trim off yarn ends.

STITCH AND ROW COUNTER

This is a small drum-shaped counter that slides up to the top of the needle shaft. It is twisted to move the numerals on and keep count of numbers of stitches.

> ### Insight
> Low tech: mark groups of pattern rows on paper and cross them off as you go.
>
> High tech: a digital sports lap counter is great for keeping track of your rows.

POINT PROTECTORS

Rubber or plastic stoppers go onto the needle ends when you are not knitting. These prevent the stitches from coming off the needles and will protect a knitting bag from being accidentally punctured.

MARKERS

These are small coloured rings used to mark the beginning of a row when knitting in the round on a set of double-pointed needles or a circular needle.

Eco and ethical yarns and needles

We are all much more aware of where our food and goods come from now, and are encouraged to scan labels for countries of origin, ethical credentials, chemical content, growing and production methods. It makes sense that those who are sensitive to these issues will also want to know that they are using yarns that adhere to their own high standards and codes of practice. Consumer pressure has brought change, and many familiar big name brands now have organic wool and cotton yarn ranges. Sheep and alpaca farmers offer locally produced yarns that have a smaller carbon footprint, and natural yarns that add no chemical dyes to the environment. Recycled yarns are spun from silk, cotton and rayon in the Far East, and there are now yarns made from fast-growing hemp, bamboo and corn that have similar qualities to cotton. An ethical Vietnamese company, Lantern Moon, makes fine knitting needles from wood and bamboo that are in demand worldwide because they are a joy to knit with and the company is known to support the communities where they are made. It makes sense to consider all these issues.

Materials

Insight

Yarn labels carry key information such as what needle size to choose, the yarn weight and the dye lot number. The washing instructions and the yarn's place of origin should also be there, along with the brand's contact details.

Knitting yarns come in many different weights and textures. They can be manmade or natural or a mixture of the two.

Natural fleece yarns are manufactured from sheep's wool, alpaca from llama's wool, cashmere and mohair from goats' hair and angora from rabbits' hair.

The natural plant yarns are cotton or linen made from flax or silk spun by silkworms that dine on mulberry leaves. Viscose and rayon have vaguely natural credentials as they are made from wood pulp that has to go through complex chemical processes to produce a yarn from cellulose.

Natural yarns are comfortable to wear next to the skin. Knitted cotton feels heavier than wool and is great for children's garments as they often complain that wool is itchy.

Insight

British yarn producers adhere to strict animal welfare and environmental standards. Look for the Fairtrade mark on imported yarns. Cheap imports come at a price!

Wool and cotton mixtures are a good compromise as they have all the best qualities of both yarns.

Mohair is soft and fluffy and feels quite glamorous. The wool is inclined to shed fibres. Mohair gives warmth without weight.

Angora is fluffy, too, but the shorter pile means it is less likely to shed. It is extremely feminine in character.

Alpaca is the new kid on the block in the UK. Alpacas seem to like our climate. The yarn is generally soft, but textures vary, as do proportions of synthetics added in imported yarns. Baby alpaca is beautifully soft.

Silk has a surprisingly rough texture on its own and is exceptionally hard wearing. Fine spun and mixed with other yarns such as cashmere it becomes soft and luxurious.

Cashmere is simply the softest, warmest and lightest of all. Even 5% cashmere will make a noticeable difference to the feel of a yarn.

Synthetic or manmade yarns are never as warm as their natural equivalents, but they have the big advantage of not shrinking, being easy to wash and dry and keeping their shape and colour. Children often prefer their feel.

Mixing a small percentage of synthetic yarn into cotton or wool can lend the yarn these same qualities without sacrificing its natural credentials.

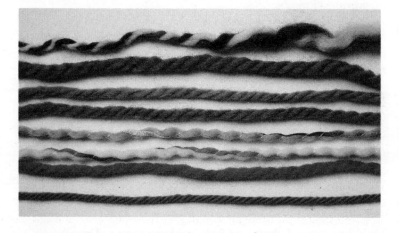

FANCY YARNS

Bouclé, chenille and metallic yarns have been around for a long time, but the recent knitting boom has a lot to do with the invention of new fashion yarns such as eyelash, which knits up to look like fur, raggy yarn with knots and irregularities, and cotton tape, which is broad and flat and is knitted on large needles to make airy summer garments and accessories.

MOST FAMILIAR YARNS

▶ *2, 3 and 4 ply – fine yarn, 2–3.5 mm needles*
▶ *Sock wool – ultrafine yarn, 2–3 mm needles*
▶ *Double knitting (DK) – versatile, medium-weight easy knitting yarn, 4–5 mm needles*
▶ *Chunky – about double the weight of DK, 6–8 mm*
▶ *Super chunky – double the weight of chunky size, 10–15 mm needles.*

Note

The projects in the following chapters assume that the reader has a basic knowledge of knitting. Where specific stitches or other techniques (e.g. making a pompom) are required, instructions are included in the chapter. For guidance on the basics of knitting (e.g. casting on, basic knitting techniques and stitches, knitting abbreviations) and other hints and tips please turn to the Appendix, which contains a wealth of useful information and advice.

2

A garter stitch scarf

As soon as you have learned to hold the wool and the needles comfortably and can do the basic knit stitch, you are ready to knit a scarf. Plain knit garter stitch is ideal for scarves because it knits up flat and has plenty of stretch.

A simple hand-knitted scarf is comforting in a way that a bought one could never be, and if you make a nice long one you will be practising and improving your knitting rhythm and making something at the same time. The more you knit in each knitting session the better your scarf will look, because the tension relaxes and becomes more even with repetition and this will create a nice even texture.

The scarf shown in Figure 2.2 is 140 cm long by 15 cm wide. Reduce the number of stitches to make a narrower version, use more yarn and knit more rows to make it longer.

Materials
Three 50 g balls of chunky yarn
5–6 m chunky yarn to match or contrast

Equipment
Pair 7 mm needles
Large crochet hook for the fringe

A scarf knitted with chunky wool on size 6–7 mm needles is a quick, easy and encouraging first project. The fringing is entirely optional – some like it and some don't.

Garter stitch

This can be worked on any number of stitches.

Row 1: k.

Garter stitch is made by using the knit or plain stitch (see pages 118–119) to work every row. The effect is one of ridged wavy lines and it looks the same on both sides.

It stretches both ways and is the starting point for all knitters.

The same effect can be achieved by knitting all rows in purl stitch.

Garter stitch lies flat and is useful for creating borders.

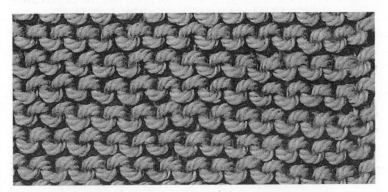

Figure 2.1 Garter stitch.

Insight

Always join a new ball of yarn at the start of a row, not in the middle. If you add stripes of colour to this scarf, the ends will have to be woven in later. To make them invisible, follow the direction of the stitches with your needle, weaving it back about 6 stitches along the row, then snip off the ends.

Knitting the scarf

TENSION

12 stitches over 12 rows to make a 10 cm square.

PATTERN

Cast on 18 stitches.

K all rows.

Keep tension moderately loose so that the stitches stay on the needle but can slide along it easily.

Cast off loosely.

Figure 2.2 Keep a friend warm in winter.

Adding a fringe

Cut multiple strands of yarn into twice the depth you want for the fringe. These are 40 cm in length to create a 20 cm fringe.

Divide them into groups of three strands and fold these in half.

Use the crochet hook to draw the folded ends through spaces between stitches in the row above the cast-off edge and make a loop.

Use the crochet hook to draw the long strands through this loop. Pull them up firmly to make a knot at the top.

Repeat this at regular intervals along the same side of the work.

Trim with sharp scissors to level the fringe.

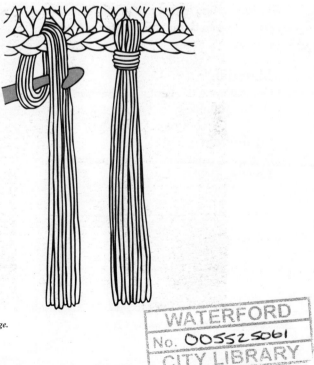

Figure 2.3 Making a fringe.

3

A striped cotton shoulder bag

Choose nice chunky cotton yarn and two or more of your
favourite colours to knit yourself a funky new bag. The bag is
worked in a single piece, starting at the bottom on long needles
and knitting it as deep as you like, then casting off on both sides
to work on eight remaining stitches in the middle, which form
the strap.

The bag is then folded in half and sewn along the base and side
seam. The end of the strap is stitched in place across the top of the
side seam.

> **Materials**
> One ball each of chunky cotton yarn in orange and lime.
> Or use a double strand of any DK hand-knitting cotton.
>
> **Equipment**
> Pair 5 mm needles
> Tapestry needle

Knitting the bag

TENSION

15 stitches over 15 rows to make a 10 cm square.

Figure 3.1 *Garter stitch has a thick rippled texture.*

PATTERN

Cast on 50 stitches using the green yarn.

Work in knit stitch throughout, keeping the tension as even as you can.

K six rows.

*Leave the green yarn at the edge and k the next two rows with the orange yarn. Now leave this yarn at the edge.

Pick up the green yarn and k the next two rows in green and leave it again.

Pick up the orange yarn and k the next two rows then break the yarn*.

Pick up the green and continue knitting with it for the next 10 rows.

Now repeat from * – *.
K another 10 rows using the green yarn.
Repeat from * – *.

K a further two rows of green then cast off 22 stitches, k the
following eight stitches and cast off the remaining 22 stitches.

Rejoin the work using the green yarn and k a further 84 rows on
the eight stitches to make the shoulder strap. The strap can be
made firmer if you knit into the back of the loop to make a twisted
knit stitch, rather than knitting into the front in the usual way.

Making up

Block and press the bag (see pages 140–142).

Thread a length of green cotton onto a wide-eyed needle and sew
up the bag, beginning at the top and working down the side seam
and across the base. Secure the yarn and weave it into the work.
Stitch the strap securely to the top of the bag so that it sits across
the side seam. Weave the remaining thread into the knitting on the
inside of the bag.

ADDING A LINING

The bag will be even more useful if you make a cotton lining.

Add 4 cm both ways to the actual measurements of the bag.

Cut out two pieces of fabric according to those measurements.

Stitch them together leaving the top end open.

Keep the raw edges on the outside and slip the lining inside the bag.

The top edge seam can be folded in towards the knitting and
slipstitched to the inside top edge of the bag.

4

A chunky knit cushion cover

Big needles and super chunky wool mean that one of these stylish cushion covers can be made in an evening. The pure wool used here creates an invitingly soft and luxurious place to rest your head. Simple stocking stitch gives a smooth finish and the garter stitch flap adds a textural contrast. Make sure the buttons are large enough to suit the cushion proportions.

Materials
Three 100 g balls of super chunky wool in a rust colour
3 large buttons

Equipment
Pair 12 mm needles
Tapestry needle

Insight
Use a good-quality yarn for the cushion cover because you may want to rest your head on it.

Stocking stitch

Stocking stitch is made by knitting and purling alternate rows. One row knit is followed by one row purl to give a smooth surface on one side, usually the front, and a pebbled one on the back. It can be worked on any number of stitches.

Row 1: k.
Row 2: p.

Figure 4.1 Stocking stitch.

Knitting the cushion cover

TENSION

8 stitches over 10 rows to make a 10 cm square.

PATTERN

Cast on 34 stitches.

Row 1: k.
Row 2: p.

Repeat till the work measures 68 cm (about 70 rows).

Change to garter stitch (see page 19) and k four rows.

Basketweave stitch (see pages 126–127) on large needles with super chunky yarn is a good pattern variation for this cushion cover.

BUTTONHOLE ROWS

Row 1: cast off 4 k7 cast off 4 k7 cast off 4 k4.
Row 2: k4 cast on 4 k7 cast on 4 k7 cast on 4 k4.
Tip: It is easier to cast on mid-row if you turn the work, cast on, then turn back to continue.

K another four rows and cast off loosely.

Figure 4.2 Large vintage buttons give a stylish finish.

Making up

Block and press very lightly (see pages 140–142).

> **Insight**
> Stocking stitch curls up at the side edges, which makes it hard
> to see which stitches you need to pick up. Place a damp cloth
> over your knitting and press gently with a warm iron. Once
> flat the edge stitches will be more obvious.

Turn the cover inside out and sew up the side seams using
backstitch.

Mark the positions for the buttons and use a finer yarn to stitch
them in place.

Fill the cover with a cushion pad and ... relax.

A ski hat with a pompom

There is something undeniably cute about a knitted hat with a pompom – especially when the pompom is as large and sassy as this one. The hat is knitted on four needles, which can seem a bit unwieldy at the beginning but using chunky wool ensures that it grows quickly. Four-needle knitting is easier once you have knitted a few rows, so don't give up – persevere and you will soon get into the rhythm of it.

This project is all in rib stitch.

Materials
Two 50 g balls chunky bright pink wool
Two 50 g balls chunky white wool

Equipment
Set of four double-pointed 6 mm needles
Tapestry needle
Two 12 cm circles of card (cereal boxes are ideal)
Pair of sharp scissors

Double rib stitch

This style of rib forms broader vertical stripes of raised plain and set back purl stitches. The work is identical on both sides.

Figure 5.1 A raspberry and vanilla pompom hat.

It is worked by knitting two stitches then purling two stitches to the end of the row. On the following row, the order reverses and the first two stitches are purled.

In circular knitting, the same stitches are knitted and purled in every round.

Row 1: k2 p2.
Row 2: p2 k2.

> **Insight**
>
> Double rib and reversed rib (see page 122) are useful patterns for patchwork squares. They create simple-to-knit textures that look good on both sides.

Knitting on four needles

Starting off is the most awkward part.

Cast the stitches onto a single needle first, then divide them equally between three needles. Alternatively, cast a third onto one needle, then move to a second needle and then a third, casting an equal number of stitches onto each one.

Form the needles into a triangle with the first and last stitch adjacent. Make sure that none of the cast-on edges has become twisted on the needles.

Knit the first stitch keeping the yarn as tight as possible, then continue to knit until all the first needle's stitches have been transferred to the fourth needle. Keep working around the needles in this way.

When several rows have been worked, the whole operation becomes a lot easier as it is amalgamated into a single item instead of lots of different spiky ones!

Once you have mastered holding four needles instead of two, you will discover the advantages.

One is that your work is seamless and the other is that all rows are worked on the right side in plain knit stitch but the effect is one of stocking stitch. Fairisle is usually done this way, with the different coloured yarns being stranded across on the inside of the knitting.

Garter stitch is worked as continuous purl – so the reverse to the usual applies.

To work rib in the round you should begin with a knit stitch and end with a purl stitch, and groups of stitches should not be worked across the change from one needle to another.

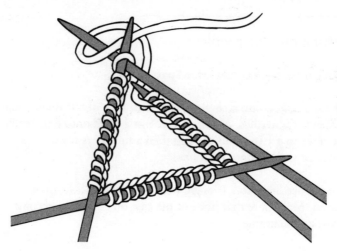

Figure 5.2 Knitting on four needles.

Insight

If you are knitting a large item, use 5 double-pointed needles instead of 4.

The stitches are equally divided over 4 needles and you knit with the fifth.

USING MARKERS

When you knit in the round, it is sometimes difficult to see where the rounds begin and this is, of course, important when you come to count them. The simplest way to keep track is to place a coloured marker in front of the first stitch and move it up the work as you knit. If you are knitting the body of a sweater it is also useful to place a marker at the halfway point so that you can distinguish the 'front' from the 'back' of the work.

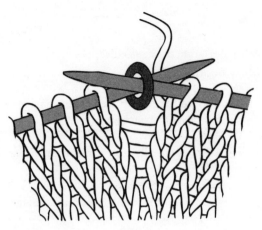

Figure 5.3 Using a marker.

Insight

If you don't have plastic ring markers, use a contrasting length of yarn as a marker – it can be snipped out later.

Knitting the hat

Abbreviations reminder

k2 p2	knit two purl two rib
k2tog	knit two together
sl1	slip one stitch

TENSION

12 stitches over 18 rows to make a 10 cm square.

PATTERN

Cast 60 stitches onto one of the needles.

Insight

I always cast on using the thumb method for hats as it gives a neat edge that is firm and stretchy.

Now divide these stitches equally over three of the needles, slipping 30 stitches onto each one.

k2 p2 rib on the next and all following rows until shaping is required.

Form the needles into a triangle and use the spare fourth needle to knit the first stitch that will join the circle.

Keep the tension quite tight for the first couple of k stitches to avoid any looping or sagging at the join. At this point you will wish you had two pairs of hands, but it will soon get easier.

Continue with this ribbing stitch until the knitting measures at least 18 cm in length.

Shaping
1st round: k2tog p2, repeat (45 stitches remain).
2nd round: p2tog k1, repeat (30 stitches remain).
3rd round: k2tog, repeat (15 stitches).
4th round: k2tog (7 stitches).

Thread the yarn onto the needle and pull the thread through the remaining seven stitches to draw the circle together and sew the yarn end into the top.

Weave any loose ends into the inside of the hat and snip off the loose ends.

Making the pompom

There is something rather magical about making pompoms. They look nothing special until you cut through the outer edge and tie them, then suddenly they emerge like fluffy day-old chicks!

Cut out two circles of card measuring 12 cm across (diameter).

Cut a 3 cm circle out of the middle of each one to make two rings.

Cut several 2 m lengths of pink and white yarn and use the needle to thread the yarn double.

Hold the two rings together as you wind the yarn evenly around them until the hole in the middle fills up.

Insert the point of the scissors at the edge between the two pieces of card and cut through the yarn all around the outside edge.

Pull the two circles just slightly apart so that you can tie a piece of yarn tightly between them, keeping these ends long enough to be used for stitching the pompom to the hat.

Cut the card away and remove it.

Fluff up the pompom and trim it to make a nice round shape, then thread the yarn and sew the pompom firmly to the top of the hat.

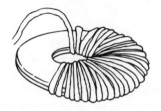

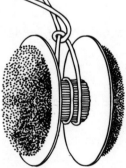

Figure 5.4 Making a pompom.

6

....

A baby's blanket

Keep a newborn baby snug and warm by knitting this simple cover that can be used on a pram, crib or tucked around a buggy. The pattern has a moss stitch border and a 'checkerboard' of stocking stitch (see pages 25–26) and reverse stocking stitch, all knitted as one piece. A handmade blanket makes a lovely gift and can be made in advance, as you don't have to consider the baby's size or to colour code it for a boy or a girl. This one was knitted in a cream DK wool on a size 5 circular needle used in the conventional way (see pages 114–116). Circular needles work well for heavier items like blankets because the weight of the knitting can rest in your lap instead of being carried on the needles.

If you would prefer to knit in a finer baby yarn, it is very important to work a tension sample and adjust the needle size for the weight of the wool.

Materials
Four 50 g balls of cream double knitting wool

Equipment
Size 4–5 circular needle
Or a pair of size 4–5 long needles

Figure 6.1 Moss stitch gives the blanket a nice flat edge.

Abbreviations reminder

k   knit
ms   moss stitch
p   purl

Reverse stocking stitch

Sometimes stocking stitch is worked the other way round and called reverse stocking stitch. This appears mostly in Aran knitting patterns where it creates more contrast between the cables, which are knitted in stocking stitch, and their background.

Row 1: p.
Row 2: k.

Ordinary moss stitch

The classic much-beloved neat stitch.

Cast on an odd number of stitches.

Row 1: *k1 p1* to last stitch k1.

Repeat this row.

....
Insight

When knitting a simple rhythmic stitch like moss stitch or single rib (see pages 121–122), it is quite easy to fall out of synch if you are interrupted mid-row. Keep checking that you are 'in pattern'. The bumpy shape is a purl stitch and 'v' shape a knit.
....

Knitting the blanket

TENSION

9 stitches and 11 rows to make a 5 cm square.

PATTERN

Cast on 80 stitches.

Row 1: k1 p1 to end of row.
Row 2: p1 k1 to end of row.

Repeat these 2 rows four times more. (10 rows moss stitch.)

For the main part of the pattern, moss stitch × 10 at beginning and end of every row.

Next row: *ms10 k15 p15 k15 p15 ms10.

Next row: ms10 p15 k15 p15 k15 ms10*.

Repeat these two rows nine times.

Next row: *ms10 p15 k15 p15 k15 ms10.

Next row: ms10 k15 p15 k15 p15 ms10*.

Repeat these two rows nine times.

Repeat these two pattern blocks three more times so that the blanket is four panels wide and eight panels long.

Work 10 rows in k1 p1 moss stitch and cast off loosely.

Making up

Weave the yarn ends into the rows and trim the ends.

Block and press the blanket using a warm iron and a damp cloth (see pages 140–142).

7

A tasselled hat for a new baby

Many of us first feel the urge to knit when we or our friends have babies. It is a fact that people who have never given knitting a thought before suddenly feel the urge to pick up a pair of needles and knit hats and booties. It must be something vaguely biological that precedes the urge to push!

Few can resist the lure of knitting in miniature as everything takes less time, less yarn and earns the most applause. Babies also look incredibly cute in beanie hats.

The instructions here are for a hat knitted on two needles with a back seam, and the style makes a feature of the natural hem rollover that happens with stocking stitch.

Materials
One 50 g ball fine baby yarn

Equipment
Pair 3.75 mm needles
Sewing-up needle
Small piece of card for the tassel

Figure 7.1 Practise your tassel-making skills.

Knitting the hat

SIZE

To fit a newborn baby 0–3 months.

TENSION

24 stitches over 32 rows to make a 10 cm square.

PATTERN

Cast on 60 stitches.

Row 1: k.
Row 2: p.

Repeat the first two rows (stocking stitch) until the work measures 15 cm, ending with a p row.

Shaping
Row 1: k8 k2tog. Repeat to end of row.
Row 2: p.
Row 3: k.
Row 4: k7 k2tog. Repeat to end of row.
Row 5: p.
Row 6: k.
Row 7: p.
Row 8: k6 k2tog. Repeat to end of row.
Row 9: p.
Row 10: k.
Row 11: p.
Row 12: k5 k2tog. Repeat to end of row.
Row 13: p.
Row 14: k.
Row 15: p.
Row 16: k4 k2tog. Repeat to end of row.
Row 17: p.
Row 18: k2tog. Repeat to end of row.
Row 19: p.
Row 20: k2tog. Repeat to end of row.

Now break off the yarn, thread the needle and draw it though the remaining stitches, overstitching the end to secure it.

Making up

Line up the two edges to be joined with the hat inside out and pin them together. Thread the yarn ends onto the sewing needle and use them to sew up the hat to within 5 cm of the bottom edge. Turn the hat the right way around and sew up the last 5 cm to the bottom edge. This gives the rollover edge at the bottom a neat finish.

The tassel

A tassel is a nice way to finish off a hat or to make a decorative zip pull.

They can be made in any length and be as fine or chunky as you like.

For this tassel, cut a piece of card 10 cm × 5 cm.

Wind the yarn around the long length of the card 20 times (less for a thinner and more for a thicker tassel). Thread the needle and draw it under the yarn at the top of the card and tie a secure knot. Remove the card, wind the threaded yarn around the top of the tassel several times to make a small ball at the top then stitch through from middle to top once or twice to secure it. Now cut the loops at the bottom and trim to a neat shape. Sew this to the top of the hat.

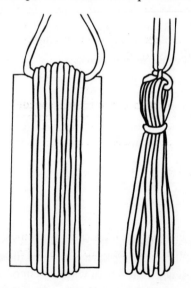

Figure 7.2 Making a tassel.

8

A child's button beanie

This child's beanie is knitted in the round on four needles (see pages 114–115). Every round is worked as knit or plain on the right side of the work but you get the effect of stocking stitch in which every alternate row is purl.

The hat rolls up around the edge and is finished off with a button on the top.

Materials
Two 50 g balls double knitting wool or cotton/wool mix
One button for the top of the hat

Equipment
Set of four double-pointed 4 mm knitting needles

Knitting the hat

SIZE

To fit a child 5–7 years. Make bigger size adjustments by increments of 10 stitches (5 cm) and add rows to the main body of the hat to adjust its depth.

TENSION

20 stitches × 32 rows to make a 10 cm square.

Figure 8.1 Practise knitting in the round.

PATTERN

Cast on 90 stitches. The thumb method will give a neat elastic edge.

Divide these evenly onto three needles so that each has 30 stitches.

Hold the needles in a triangle and use the fourth needle to begin knitting.

Pull the wool quite firmly when making the first stitch to avoid any loop forming at the join. The beginning of the round can be marked with a coloured marker ring or by noting the position of the cast-on tail end.

K in rounds until the knitting measures 14 cm.

Shaping

The hat is shaped by using the k2tog decrease at regular intervals.

Round 1: k9 k2tog. Repeat to end of row.
Round 2: k.
Round 3: k8 k2tog. Repeat to end of row.
Round 4: k.
Round 5: k7 k2tog. Repeat to end of row.
Round 6: k.
Round 7: k6 k2tog. Repeat to end of row.
Round 8: k.
Round 9: k5 k2tog. Repeat to end of row.
Round 10: k.
Round 11: k2tog. Repeat to end of row.
Round 12: k.
Round 13: k2tog. Repeat to end of row.

Making up

Break the yarn off and thread it onto a darning needle.

Thread this through the remaining stitches and pull tight to close the opening.

Stitch the ends into the wrong side of the work.

Sew a button onto the top of the hat.

A jeans-style hat

The denim yarn used for this hat is designed to fade the way jeans do, and the orange cotton detail of the hat mimics the seam stitching of blue jeans. The pattern is knitted on two needles with a back seam, but four double-pointed needles or a circular needle could be substituted if you prefer not to do any sewing up.

This hat is a beanie style with a rolled edge that doesn't cover the ears.

For those whose ears are prone to feel the cold, work the straight section at least 10 cm longer before beginning to decrease to shape the crown.

Materials
One 100 g ball of chunky denim-look wool or cotton
Small ball of orange chunky cotton yarn

Equipment
Pair 6 mm needles
Sewing-up needle

Figure 9.1 Modern wools have helped to kick-start the knitting revival.

Knitting the hat

Abbreviations reminder

k	knit
k2tog	knit two together
p	purl
st st	stocking stitch

TENSION

14 stitches and 18 rows to make a 10 cm square.

PATTERN

Use the thumb method to cast on 72 stitches.

Try to master the thumb method as it makes a firm but stretchy edging ideal for hats.

Row 1: k.
Row 2: p.

Repeat these rows working in st st until the work measures 14 cm from the start, ending on a knit row. Break the yarn.

*Work the p row using the orange cotton then break the yarn.

Rejoin the denim yarn*.

Work a further five rows st st ending with a k row.

Break the yarn.

Repeat * – *.

K five rows of st st ending with a p row.

Shaping
Row 1: k1 *k12 k2tog (×5)* k1 (67 stitches remain).
Row 2: p.
Row 3: k1 *k11 k2tog (×5)* k1 (62 stitches remain).
Row 4: p.
Row 5: k1 *k10 k2tog (×5)* k1 (57 stitches remain).
Row 6: p.
Row 7: k1 *k9 k2tog (×5)* k1 (52 stitches remain).
Row 8: p.
Row 9: k1 *k8 k2tog (×5)* k1 (47 stitches remain).
Row 10: p.
Row 11: k1 *k7 k2tog (×5)* k1 (42 stitches remain).
Row 12: p.
Row 13: k1 *k2tog (×20)* k1 (22 stitches remain).
Row 14: p.
Row 15: k2tog (×11).

Break the yarn and thread the wool through the remaining stitches and pull them firmly together.

Stitch the end to secure it on the wrong side of the crown.

Making up

Use a large sewing-up needle to weave all the yarn ends into the inside of the hat and sew up the back seam neatly, stitching on the right side for the last 3 cm or 4 cm where the rim rolls over.

Baby toys

Small babies will love these soft textures and bright shapes. If you are making all three toys buy six different colours of yarn; otherwise use up oddments of washable baby-friendly yarn. If you would like to add noise to the toys, put a few dry beans inside a plastic film canister and bury it in the middle of the filling.

Insight

The baby toys don't take long to knit and they make such a change from all the mass-produced rattles and balls. Try knitting or embroidering initials on the cube as a special present for a newborn.

The ball

This ball has a diameter of 14 cm.

Materials
Six different coloured balls of cotton DK yarn
Washable toy filling

Equipment
Pair size 3.75 mm needles
Pair of scissors
Sewing-up needle

Figure 10.1 Simple shapes for baby's hands.

PATTERN

Cast on two stitches.

Row 1: p.
Row 2: cast on 1 k2 cast on 1 (4 stitches).
Row 3: p.
Row 4: cast on 1 k4 cast on 1 (6 stitches).
Row 5: p.
Row 6: cast on 1 k6 cast on 1 (8 stitches).
Row 7: p.
Row 8: cast on 1 k8 cast on 1 (10 stitches).
Row 9: p.
Row 10: cast on 1 k10 cast on 1 (12 stitches).

Work eight rows in st st (k one row p one row).

Continue in stocking stitch, but k2tog at the beginning and end of every knit row until only one stitch remains.

Break the yarn, leaving it long enough to sew up the side, thread it through the loop and pull it up tight.

Change colour and knit five more shapes the same as this.

MAKING UP

Use the yarn ends to sew sections of the ball together on the wrong side. When only one seam remains sew halfway, turn the ball right side out and stuff the ball with the filling. Don't be mean with it, as the fuller it is the better the shape will be.

Sew up the last section of seam neatly from the outside and poke the needle through the ball to hide the yarn end safely inside.

The cube

This cube has been knitted in plain colours, but even more fun can be had by knitting coloured stripes, creating different pattern textures or knitting motifs or letters. This is quite a large cube and the size can easily be adjusted by using fewer stitches to make the squares.

Materials
Six different coloured cotton DK yarns
Washable toy filling

Equipment
Pair 3.75 mm needles
Sewing-up needle

PATTERN

The cube's sides measure 12 cm × 12 cm.

Cast on 24 stitches.

Row 1: k.
Row 2: p.

Repeat these two rows 16–18 more times, depending on your tension.

When the shape is square, cast off.

Break the yarn, leaving it long enough to sew up the side, thread it through the loop and pull it up tight.

Repeat five more times, using a different colour for each one.

MAKING UP

Use the yarn ends and matching yarns to sew the sides of the cube together, on the wrong side, leaving half of one side open.

Turn the cube right side out and stuff it with the filling.

Finally, sew up the seam neatly on the outside and poke the needle through to hide the yarn end inside the cube.

The pyramid

One square and four triangles are knitted to make a sturdy pyramid. The sides can either be worked on stitches picked up from the edges of the square base or they can be knitted as individual triangles to be sewn to the base afterwards. The individual method is described here.

Materials
Five different coloured cotton DK yarns
Washable toy filling

Equipment
Pair 3.75 mm needles
Sewing-up needle

Figure 10.2 Perfect for a toy basket.

Abbreviations reminder
k   knit
k2tog   knit two together
p   purl

PATTERN

For the base: cast on 24 stitches and work a st st square as shown for the cube.

For the sides: cast on 24 stitches.

Row 1: p.
Row 2: k2tog *k*. until last two stitches k2tog.

Repeat these two rows until only one stitch remains.

Break the yarn, leaving it long enough to sew up the side, thread it through the loop and pull it up tight.

Repeat three more times using different colours.

MAKING UP

Sew all the pieces together from the wrong side, leaving half of one seam open. Turn and stuff the shape with filling.

Finally, sew up the rest of the seam neatly and poke the needle through the middle of the shape to hide the yarn end safely inside.

11

A cosy hot water bottle cover

There is nothing to beat an old-fashioned hot water bottle
for instant comfort and defrosting on a cold winter's night.
Show your hot water bottle how much you love it by knitting this
soft cabled polo neck sweater to double its huggability. Sentiment
aside, a knitted cover will prevent a hot water bottle from scalding
and also keep its heat for much longer.

Insight

Measure the width of the hot water bottle – they are not all
the same size. Enlarge or reduce the size by multiples of
2 stitches and adjust the position of the cable accordingly.

Materials
Two 50 g balls of chunky wool or wool/cashmere mix

Equipment
Pair 5.5 mm needles
Cable needle
Sewing-up needle

Figure 11.1 The ribbed neck fits snugly but will stretch to insert the hot water bottle.

Cable stitch

For basic cable stitch instructions, see pages 127–129. Here a twisted cable stitch is used.

TWISTED OR COILED ROPE STITCH

This is a bold spiral with a twist to the right.

Cast on in multiples of nine plus three.

Rows 1 and 3: *p3 k6* p3.
Rows 2, 4 and 6: *k3 p6* k3.
Row 5: *p3 slip 3 onto cable needle and leave at the back of the work k3 then k3 stitches from the cable needle* p3.

Repeat rows 1–6 as required.

Knitting the hot water bottle cover

TENSION

14 stitches over 22 rows to make a 10 cm square.

PATTERN

Front
Cast on 42 stitches.

Row 1: k18, slip three stitches onto a cable needle and hold them
at the back of the work. K the next three stitches on the left-hand
needle in the usual way then k the three stitches from the cable
needle.

Row 2: p.
Row 3: k.
Row 4: p.

Repeat rows 1–4 until the work measures 25 cm.

Shoulder shaping
Row 1: sl1 k2tog psso k to end of row.
Row 2: sl1 p2tog psso p to end of row.

Repeat these two rows. You now have 38 stitches.

Polo neck
Cast off nine stitches, then work 20 stitches in k1 p1 rib, then cast
off the nine stitches that remain on the needle.

Rejoin the wool and work 12 cm of single rib then cast off.

Row 1: k1 p1.
Row 2: k1 p1.

Making up

Sew up all the seams apart from the polo-neck opening.

Fold an empty hot water bottle in half and insert it through the stretchy neck opening.

Carefully fill with hot water and snuggle up.

....

A child's Cornish-style sweater

'Gansey' patterns initially appear more complex than they are when broken down into their component parts. This one is no exception. This fisherman's-style sweater for a young child has been designed to practise stitches and techniques described in the book.

The panels are stocking stitch, moss, grille, rib and a very simple cable section all framed inside a garter stitch border.

The wide shape will allow a wriggly toddler plenty of room to manoeuvre and the generous neck opening will make it easy to get on and off.

> ## Materials
> Seven 50 g balls of 4 ply wool/cotton mix
>
> ## Equipment
> Three 3.25 mm needles
> 3.25 mm circular needle
> Two large stitch holders
> Medium-sized cable needle

Knitting the sweater

Abbreviation reminder

m1   make one – increase by knitting into both front and back of next stitch

Figure 12.1 Practise your cable stitch.

SIZE

To fit a child aged 2–3 years.

The neck and chest measurements are generous. To make the garment for a 4 year old, increase the length of the sleeves and body by increasing the number of rows knitted in the stocking stitch sections of the front, back and sleeves.

MEASUREMENTS

Shoulder to hem: 36 cm
Sleeves: 25 cm
Across chest: 34 cm
Across back: 34 cm
Around neck: 40 cm

TENSION

28 stitches and 36 rows to make a 10 cm square.

PATTERN

Back and front
Cast on 78 stitches using 3.25 mm needles and work 10 rows garter stitch (see page 19).

Work four rows of k2 p2 rib, keeping the first and last six stitches k.

Continue working in st st until the work measures 22 cm, keeping the first six and last six stitches k and ending with a p row.

Commence pattern.

MOSS STITCH PANEL
Row 1: k6 *k1 p1* to last six stitches k6.
Row 2: k6 *p1 k1* to last six stitches k6.

Repeat these rows twice more (six rows altogether).

CABLE PANEL
Row 1: k6 *p3 k4* to last nine stitches p3 k6.
Row 2: k6 *k3 p4* to last nine stitches k9.
Row 3: as Row 1.
Row 4: as Row 2.
Row 5: k6 *p3 sl2 onto cable needle and leave at the back of work k2 then k2 from the cable needle*. Repeat to last nine stitches p3 k6.
Row 6: as row 2.

Repeat these six rows three times (18 rows altogether).

Stocking stitch the next four rows, keeping the first and last six stitches k.

GRILLE STITCH PANEL

This version of moss stitch appears complex but is actually very easy to knit. It has a strong raised squared pattern running over a moss stitch background.

The pattern is worked over four rows and a stitch counter is recommended.

Cast on an odd number of stitches.

Row 1: k to the end.
Row 2: k to the end.
Row 3: *k1 p1* to last stitch k1.
Row 4: k1 p1 to the end.

For this sweater:

Row 1: k.
Row 2: k.
Row 3: k6 *k1 p1* to last six stitches k.
Row 4: k6 *k1 p1* to last six stitches k.

Repeat these four rows four times.

Do not cast off; keep stitches on the needle.

Sleeves (make two!)
Cast on 40 stitches using 3.25 needles.

K1 row.

Work in k2 p2 rib until work measures 5 cm.

SHAPING
Continue in st st as follows:

Next row: k2 m1 knit to last two stitches m1 k2.

Work one row.

Increase as before on next and then every fourth row until there are 68 stitches on the needle.

Continue in st st without further shaping until the work measures 21 cm from beginning.

Next row: k2 p2 rib to end.

Repeat this row six times.

Cast off in k.

Insight

Young children's heads are large for their bodies, so it is advisable to measure for the neck opening and, if in doubt, make it larger. If you work the cast-off row loosely this will give the opening plenty of stretch.

Shoulders and neck

The shoulders are joined by knitting the back and front sections together using a third needle. Line up the two pieces of knitting with the needle points facing the same way and the wrong sides facing each other.

K2tog through first two loops taking one stitch from each needle.

Repeat with next two loops again taking one stitch from each needle.

Cast off first stitch.

Continue in this way until 14 stitches have been cast off from each needle.

Break off the yarn and slip next 50 stitches from front onto a stitch holder.

Slip 50 stitches from the back onto another stitch holder.

Rejoin wool and work the second shoulder as before.

Slip stitches from both holders onto the circular needle (100 stitches altogether).

Knit eight rounds of k2 p2 rib, casting off loosely in rib.

Making up

Block and press lightly.

Sew sleeves into the armholes, matching the centre of the sleeve with the shoulder seam.

Join side seams and sleeve seams together using a backstitch.

Leave the garter stitch rows at the hem open to form a split.

13

Dishcloth patterns

You want me to knit a dishcloth? 'Life's too short', I hear you cry! I say, give it a try.

All of us get through mountains of washing-up cloths, sponges and brushes in the course of our lifetime, using them every day with little or no thought to what they look like or how long they last.

Knitted cotton cloths are different. They do the job really well because they are absorbent; rough cotton is strong and mildly abrasive; they can be put through the washing machine to freshen up and the openwork patterns allow air to circulate through so that they also dry easily. And being made of natural cotton they are less likely to be whiffy.

This is also an ideal way to practise your lacy and openwork knitting patterns.

Dishcloths and washcloths don't have to be very big and you will find that even complex patterns that require intense concentration will not take very long to knit.

Make them for friends and you will be amazed at how much they are appreciated. And the better they look, the happier you will feel when you do those dishes …

Knitting dishcloths can be a positive life-enhancing experience!

Spread the word.

Figure 13.1 Practise your openwork knitting stitches.

Turkish openwork cloth

This is also known as Turkish faggoting. It is a deceptively fancy openwork stitch that is easily learned. It is worked as a single repeated pattern row on an even number of stitches until the required length is reached.

Bands of garter stitch are worked within the cloth help to keep the square shape.

Materials
One ball of dishcloth cotton

Equipment
Pair of 5 mm needles
Use large sizes to make bigger holes or smaller for a tighter texture

PATTERN

Cast on 40 stitches quite loosely.

Row 1: k1 *yfwd k2tog*. Repeat to last stitch k1.

Repeat this row to form the main pattern.

Work five more rows of pattern then six rows of garter stitch or plain knitting.

Work 18 pattern rows then six rows of garter stitch.

Work six rows of pattern and cast off loosely.

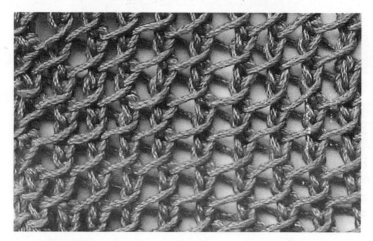

Figure 13.2 Turkish fagotting.

Lace rib cloth

This is a lovely stitch for a baby blanket or a throw. It also makes a very pretty patterned cloth with a scalloped edge, and would make

a nice facecloth but it would need to be knitted in a softer DK
cotton yarn.

Insight

This project would be ideal for trying out one of the organic
cotton yarns. There is a list of suppliers in 'Taking it further'
(see pages 92–95).

Once again, and surprisingly as it appears very complex, the
pattern is worked as a single row with a purl row between that
gives you a chance to pick up speed and take your eyes off the
knitting.

Materials

One ball of dishcloth cotton or soft DK cotton for a facecloth

Equipment

Pair 4–5 mm needles (the smaller size gives a tighter texture)

PATTERN

The pattern is worked as any number of stitches divisible by
10 plus one extra stitch.

Cast on 41 stitches.

Row 1: k1 *yrn k3 sl1 k2tog psso k2 yrn k1*. Repeat to end.
Row 2: p.

Repeat these two rows until you have knitted a square, then cast
off loosely.

Insight

Lace rib can be given a more open style by purling into
the back instead of the front of the slipped stitch from the
previous row.

Figure 13.3 Lace rib.

Garter stitch pot holder

Protect your hands when lifting something hot in the kitchen by using one of these thick cotton pot holders. The yarn is used double here to add bulk to the knitting.

Materials
One ball of dishcloth cotton

Equipment
Pair 4–5 mm needles (the smaller size makes a denser fabric)

PATTERN

Unwind half the cotton ball and rewind to give you two smaller balls.

Cast on 30 stitches using both balls to double the yarn thickness.

Knit 24 rows in garter stitch, then cast off.

Betty Martin pattern

Betty Martin was a Guernsey knitter who gave her name to this simple but effective pattern. It is not strictly openwork but has a good texture and is fun to knit. This pattern would have been used on fishermen's sweaters, but it adapts well to the dishcloth format. The edges are picked up and knitted with stitch increases at the corners.

Materials
Dishcloth cotton

Equipment
Pair 4 mm needles
Sewing-up needle for loose ends

PATTERN

Cast on a multiple of four stitches plus two more.

Row 1: k.
Row 2: p.
Row 3: *k2 p2* to last two stitches, k2.
Row 4: *p2 k2* to last two stitches, p2.

Repeat this sequence until you have a nice square cloth.

Edging
Pick up and knit an equal even number of stitches from one edge.

Row 1: cast on one stitch then k to the end and cast on one extra stitch.
Row 2: k to end.

Repeat these two rows twice more and cast off.

Repeat on the other three sides then stitch up the corners and weave the loose ends into the fabric of the cloth.

14

A beach bag or large shopper

This large bag is knitted using mesh stitch with cotton tape on big needles. Decide on a shopping or beach trip and knit the bag you need in a couple of days. The openwork style makes this particularly good for carrying damp beach clothes and towels. This number of stitches makes a big 40 cm × 40 cm bag but the same pattern can be used to make a smaller version – simply cast on fewer stitches and follow the same instructions.

The bag is very easy to line. Simply cut two pieces of fabric to match the bag size and machine stitch side and base seams. Turn a hem over at the top and slipstitch it to the inside top edge of the knitted bag.

Knitted handles have a tendency to stretch, but that can be prevented by lining the handle in fabric or ribbon.

Insight
The unlined bag will expand to carry more than you'd expect. If you add a lining you lose this feature, but it is still a good idea to either line the strap or reduce the number of rows knitted if you like a shortish strap. It does stretch without a lining.

Materials
Five 50 g balls of chunky cotton tape

Equipment
Pair 10 mm needles for the bag
Pair 7 mm needles for the strap
Very large sewing-up needle

Abbreviations reminder

garter stitch	every row k
moss stitch	row 1: k1 p1; row 2: p1 k1
psso	pass slipped stitch over
sl1	slip one stitch
yon	yarn over needle

Beginner's guide to mesh stitch

This is a wide mesh worked as a single repeated pattern row, on an even number of stitches.

Cast on loosely.

Wrap yarn around the needle once from, then back to, the knit position.

Slip a stitch k1.

Lift the slipped stitch over the knit stitch and off the needle psso.

Figure 14.1 Cotton tape makes an attractive mesh.

Knitting the bag

PATTERN

Cast on 50 stitches.

Row 1: *yon sl1 k1 psso*.

Try to complete each row without interruptions, but if you do have to stop you can see whether your last stitch is a wrapped or knitted one. Wrapped stitches slant whereas knitted ones sit straight on the needle.

Repeat this pattern row until the work measures 38 cm.

Now k next four rows (plain knitting) then cast off loosely.

Knit another piece in the same way.

Strap
Using the 7 mm needles, cast on eight stitches and work six rows of moss stitch.

Row 1: k1 p1.
Row 2: p1 k1.

Change to garter stitch until work measures 55 cm.

Now work six rows in moss stitch and cast off.

Making up

Thread a long length of cotton tape onto the needle and sew up three sides of the bag.

Stitch the strap to the sides so that the strap straddles the joined edges.

OPTIONAL LINING INSTRUCTIONS

Lay the bag on a sheet of newspaper and draw the shape, adding a 4 cm seam allowance, then, using this as a template, cut two pieces of fabric to line the bag and a long strip to line the strap. Make a French seam by sewing close to the edge on the right side to join the fabric pieces, then, turning them the other way out, press the seams and sew another seam 1 cm from the edge. This tucks away all the raw edges and prevents fraying.

The lining can now be put inside the bag and hem stitched along the top inside edge. The strap lining can either be machined by sewing with the fabric side upwards or simply hem stitched to the knitted strap and the top of the lining fabric.

15

A make-up purse

Knit a pretty and practical make-up purse in washable cotton in stocking stitch with a decorative heart pattern. The purse is triangular in shape so that it sits flat on a dressing table, and it is compact enough to carry around in your handbag.

The hearts are worked from the chart provided, where every square represents a stitch. This one has been fitted with a light cotton lining and a zip. The purse can also be left unlined with the zip slipstitched into the knitted edge.

If you have not knitted a motif like this before, it is a good idea to do a practice square.

The knack of making successful mid-row colour changes is to concentrate on keeping the same yarn tension as you do for the rest of the knitting, otherwise the heart shape will distort. Too loose and the shape will be baggy, too tight and it will appear pinched.

Insight

Not ready for Fairisle? Use Swiss darning to add motifs to stocking stitch by sewing over the knitted stitches in a contrasting yarn. Follow the direction of each stitch with the needle and don't pull the yarn too tightly.

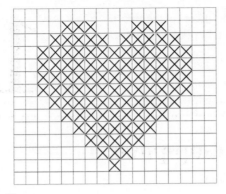

Figure 15.1 Heart motif.

Materials
Knitted in twisted glazed 3 ply cotton
Two balls bright pink
One ball cream

Equipment
Pair 3.25 mm needles

Knitting the purse

TENSION

24 stitches over 32 rows to make a 10 cm square.

PATTERN

Base
Cast on 67 stitches.

Row 1: k.
Row 2: p.

Continue work in st st for 12 cm and cast off.

Triangular end piece (make two!)
Cast on 28 stitches in bright pink.

Row 1: k.
Row 2: p.
Row 3: k1 k2tog k to last three stitches then k2tog and k1.
Row 4: p.

Repeat 3rd and 4th rows until four stitches remain, then cast off.

Sides (make two!)
Cast on 67 stitches.

Row 1: k.
Row 2: p.

Repeat these two rows (st st) for eight rows.

Begin heart pattern detail: k13 stitches, then insert pattern as shown on the chart, then k13 stitches to the end of the row.

Follow the pattern as shown on the chart.

Work another eight rows st st and cast off.

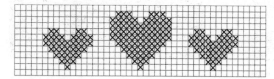

Figure 15.2 Make-up bag chart.

MAKING UP

Making the lining
Block and press the individual knitted pieces (see pages 140–142).
Draw a paper pattern of each of the shapes (2 × ends; 1 × base;

2 × sides), add a 2 cm seam allowance and cut out a cotton lining. Machine stitch the seams, leaving the long top seam open.

Making up the purse
Lay the two long side pieces flat and pin the zip between them. Stitch the zip in place before making up the purse. Now stitch the ends to the sides. Undo the zip and turn the work inside out and stitch the base in place. Turn the work again so that it is right side out.

Fitting the lining
Turn the lining so that the seams are on the outside and place it inside the knitted purse. Turn over a small hem, tucking it between the lining and the knitting, and slipstitch the lining in place.

Figure 15.3 Pretty and practical – and all your own work.

16

....

A siesta pillow

Use this whenever you want to take a catnap.

This little cushion would make a perfect gift for a friend who is inclined to take a little siesta after lunch. The pattern is easy to knit and the alphabet is a very simple one suitable for a beginner. The two colours used here create a vibrant contrast (a bit more fiesta than siesta) but the effect can be softened by choosing softer, harmonizing colours like pink and lilac.

Materials
Two 50 g balls of main colour red 4 ply mercerized cotton
One 50 g ball of pattern colour blue 4 ply mercerized cotton
30 cm × 20 cm cushion pad or fabric and polyester/kapok filling

Equipment
Pair 3.25 mm needles
Sewing-up needle

Knitting the pillow

SIZE

Makes a 30 cm × 20 cm cushion cover.

TENSION

24 stitches over 29 rows to make a 10 cm square.

Abbreviations reminder

k   knit
p   purl
Rs   right side facing
st st   stocking stitch

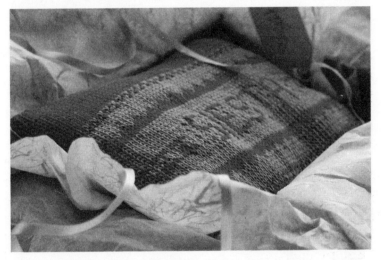

Figure 16.1 Somewhere for a friend to rest their head.

PATTERN

Red colour = A.
Blue colour = B.

Front

Using A, cast on 71 stitches.

Work 4 cm in st st, beginning with a k row finishing on a p row.

Row 1: Rs *k1A k1B*. Repeat to end of row.
Row 2: p1B p1A. Repeat to end of row.

Work four rows st st in B.

Row 3: k1A k3B. Repeat to end of row.
Row 4: p1B *p1A p3B*. Repeat to end of row.
Row 4: kA.
Row 5: pA.

Work four rows in st st in B.

Use the chart for the following nine rows to knit 'zzz SIESTA zzz'.

Each square represents one stitch.

Work four rows in st st in B.

Row 15: pA.
Row 16: kA.
Row 17: p3A p1B. Repeat to end of row.
Row 18: k1B *k1A k3B*. Repeat to end of row.

Work four rows in st st in B.

Row 19: p1A p1B. Repeat to end of row.
Row 20: k1B k1A. Repeat to end of row.

Work 4 cm in st st in A and cast off.

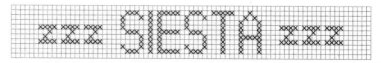

Figure 16.2 Siesta pillow chart.

Back
Cast on 72 stitches and work in st st in A until work measures 20 cm.

Measure it against the front and adjust by adding or subtracting a row or two if necessary, then cast off.

MAKING UP

Block and press the two pieces.

Join one short side and two long sides, then insert the cushion pad and stitch the last side neatly.

Now ... take a nap. You've earned it after these projects!

Taking it further

Knitting together

Knitting as a group activity seems a strange concept until you try it, then you understand and realize what has been missing from your life.

Knitting groups are for busy people who do not usually justify taking time for themselves. These multi-taskers are often too caught up with their jobs/partners/homes/gardens/kids/chores to spend a couple of relaxing hours chatting to friends. They are also for people who spend too many evenings on their own but dislike the formality of joining a class or a club.

Knitting is a great leveller. We all begin with a pair of needles, a ball of wool – and a vision. The knitting, as is true of most repetitive activities, soon becomes automatic and we find that our minds relax and are freed up for conversation.

We become passengers on each other's train of thoughts.

STARTING UP A KNITTING GROUP

Knitting groups have achieved almost cult status in the USA and the trend has grown into a worldwide phenomenon. Don't let that put you off the idea of starting up a new group though, because there is no shame in being part of something fashionable when it is also positive, non-competitive and, essentially, life enhancing.

The way you start a group will depend on where you live and how you spend the rest of your time. If you already know people who knit, try suggesting that you start a group together.

Designate one evening a week or fortnight as 'knitnight', with a change of venue each week from one home to another. The only requirement is comfy seats and enough elbow room to accommodate about 10 knitters. You do not need fees or agendas, simply arrive at any time after 7.30 and leave by 11.

Refreshments are optional and could be a glass of wine or juice to quench the thirst and a cup of tea or wickedly indulgent hot chocolate towards the end of the evening. Sometimes the numbers will swell and then shrink down to three or four, which will be quieter but no less enjoyable. There will be quiet moments when the only sound is that of clicking needles, but more often than not there will be several animated conversations going on at the same time. And a lot of laughter!

Start-up suggestions

1   *Put a notice in your local wool shop window or a poster on a work, college or school noticeboard.*
2   *Join a knitting forum on the web, such as UK Handknitters (a Yahoo! group), www.knit-today.com or Phoenix Knitters at www.knittingforums.org.uk where there is online chat, knitting-related news, shared ideas, problem solving and topics for discussion. Put out feelers about knitting in your area via one of these.*
3   *Wear a homemade 'Join my knitting group' badge and wait for enquiries.*
4   *Advertise in the 'What's On' section of your local paper.*
5   *Teach people you like to knit – supply a ball of wool and needles with stitches already cast on to make a garter stitch square for a blanket.*
6   *Approach a coffee shop or bar with the idea of a weekly or monthly knit-in.*
7   *Pick a day or evening that suits most of you most of the time. Be decisive but not too rigid – remember, this is about having fun!*
8   *Don't over-recruit. If the group is to meet in members' homes, try to limit it to a number that most can accommodate comfortably. Be flexible and inclusive though – there will be times when only a few can make it and this is an ideal time for a smaller home to be used.*

9 *Try to include a wide age range. Older members are likely to be more experienced and the younger ones more experimental and arty.*

10 *Support a charity knitting project. There are 'scarves for the homeless' and 'hats for the premature baby unit' projects in many cities. Once again, an online search will reveal a cause close to your heart. In our group, we knit simple baby vests for a Ugandan maternity hospital. This way everyone who joins has a garment to knit from dayone.*

KEEPING IT GOING

Once you have started a group and had a few get-togethers, it will become clear that some core members will find it more convenient to host the evenings, while others look forward to getting out of the house. It is important that people feel neither put upon nor left out – the way we do it is to decide at the end of each knitnight where we will be the following week. We email, text or ring each other and pass the word around. Each of us takes the responsibility of finding out for herself and, that way, nobody feels left out.

You may find that you need more structure, but we organize things in an instinctive female way and it works very well. When nobody is in charge, group decisions are quite easy. It's not a campaign you're planning – just some group knitting.

Warning
The great thing about knitting is that it isn't competitive, but catering certainly can be. Stick to the basics and only deal with thirst, not snacks. One glass of wine or water is all that's needed because our hands are knitting and our mouths are talking.

Author's experience
Initially we thought we might break for the summer, but when summer came around it seemed too conventional an idea and we just carried on as usual. And, besides, we felt we would miss the group therapy!

Knitting tips and how to progress

▶ *Once you feel comfortable with your knitting and have practised a variety of stitches, you will be ready to branch out and choose a pattern, buy the yarn and make something wonderful.*
▶ *Caution is urged! This is a make-or-break phase in your knitting future. It will be far more satisfying (and also less expensive) to knit simple garments successfully than to struggle with an over-ambitious pattern.*
▶ *Having to abandon a project is demoralizing, but we have all done it – put it on top of the wardrobe for a rainy day or hand it in at a charity shop, then start knitting something chunky for instant gratification.*
▶ *Certain things are not worth knitting. Buy a superfine cashmere sweater – it will be cheaper and look better than anything you can knit. On the other hand you can never have too many scarves.*
▶ *Knit something for a charity – it will give you a nice warm feeling inside.*
▶ *Deadlines can kill your enthusiasm for knitting. Try not to promise anything for a special date – like Christmas – when you have quite enough to do already!*

- *It is easier to knit light colours than dark – especially at night when mistakes knitted in black are virtually invisible!*
- *When you knit with pale yarn, keep the balls in a clear plastic bag loosely gathered at the top with a rubber band. The yarn will stay clean even if it drops on the floor – as it inevitably will at some stage.*
- *Yarn is dipped into containers of dye and this causes slight variations in the same colour from the different dippings. Always buy enough yarn to complete the garment, rather than buying a bit at a time. Check that the dye lot numbers are the same – every ball of yarn has one.*
- *When knitting a striped scarf from oddments, make sure that the different yarns are constructed from compatible fibres – for instance, all natural, all mixtures or all manmade fibres. Yarns behave in different ways when they are knitted up and, most importantly, when they are washed.*
- *Only substitute a large safety pin for a stitch holder for a small number of stitches or in an emergency. Safety pins can split the yarn and give you a nasty jab.*
- *Blocking and pressing: it will make all the difference if you don't rush this vital stage. Take your time and complete the sewing up with care and the results will speak for themselves.*
- *Buy shorter length needles for knitting on public transport. It will stop you poking the person next to you in the ribs.*
- *Left-handed beginners are best taught by other left-handed knitters.*
- *If the yarn doesn't slide easily along the needle, try running your needles through your hair. This adds the slightest coating of natural oil that will sort out the problem.*
- *Designate one evening a week as knitnight to knit, to sit and chat, and your friendships will grow with the rows while life stories unravel like balls of wool.*

The online knitting community

The internet is an amazing place for crafts. Its interconnectedness really appeals to knitters, who soon recognized the potential for a worldwide web of wool. A place where you can find out what you need to know, share ideas and show off your achievements to others who are genuinely interested.

It doesn't matter whether you live in a high-rise city block or out in the sticks – if you knit you can connect with other knitters. All the usual issues of being a member of a club such as location, fees, mobility, qualifications, money and age are not issues in the virtual knitting community.

It all started with a few individuals blogging about their knitting, and within five years it has totally revamped the cosy world of knitting.

There has been a huge pooling of knowledge from experts and amateurs alike and thousands of patterns are now free to download. One unexpected development is the way this virtual knitting world has brought so many like-minded people together in the real world. Become a member of the biggest online group Ravelry for instance, and you can find out who has a knitting group in your area, where and when craft events are taking place and which of your online friends will be there. They have knitting groups listed everywhere from Antartica to the Virgin Islands and there is very likely one near you too – if not, you can start one and invite members along online.

Many of the best websites and blogs are based in the USA, but no matter where you live you can get involved, ask questions, share patterns and make friends.

London knitting shop Loop also has a lovely website where you can find out about knitting groups and classes. Other great knitting sites are iKnit, Knitty, Stitch n Bitch, Yarn Harlot, Rowan Knitting Club, and to find the locations of knitting shops, classes or groups try Knit Map and join in by adding information from your local area. Subscribe to online newsfeeds from any of the big knitting sites and you receive a regular supply of emailed inspiration and all the latest on knitting yarns and accessories. And if you learn best by seeing a live demonstration there are hundreds of these on YouTube. I suggest looking at several different versions because there is no quality control and this means some demos are clearer than others.

The wonderful thing about the internet is that it is what we make of it.

www.ravelry.com
www.purlsoho.com
www.knitrowan.com
www.knitty.com
www.stitchnbitch.com
www.loopknitting.com
www.theyarnharlot.com
www.knitmap.com
www.iknit.org.uk
www.cucumberpatch.co.uk
www.knittingforums.org.uk
www.youtube.com

Yarn suppliers

DRAGON YARNS
Online suppliers of interesting pure wool ranges such as British Breeds and Bolivian alpacas.
Website: www.dragonyarns.co.uk

ROWAN YARNS
Quality yarns in gorgeous colours. Online knitting club and suppliers' information.
Green Lane Mill
Holmfirth
West Yorkshire
England
HD9 2DX
Website: www.knitrowan.com
Email: mail@knitrowan.com
Tel: 01484 681881

SIRDAR
Hand-knitting and specialist yarns.
General enquiries: enquiries@sirdar.co.uk
For stockists in your area: www.sirdar.co.uk/storelocator

TWILLEYS OF STAMFORD
Traditional yarns, handicraft cotton, denim yarn, lurex and
chunky wool.
Tel: 01780 752661
Email: twilleys@tbramsden.co.uk

JAMIESON & SMITH
Shetland wool direct from the Islands, plus patterns, kits and
a great colour range.
90 North Road
Lerwick
Shetland Isles
ZE1 0PQ
Website: www.shetlandwoolbrokers.co.uk
Tel: 01595 693579

TOFT ALPACAS
Online and onsite shop selling undyed British alpaca in a wide
shade range of natural colours – white, brown, grey, black.
Toft Manor
Toft Lane
Dunchurch
Warwickshire
CV22 6NR
Website: www.toftalpacashop.co.uk
Email: enquiries@toft-alpacas.co.uk
Tel: 01788 8106262

UK ALPACA LIMITED
Dyed British alpaca in beautiful colours or natural soft baby alpaca.
Vulscombe Farm
Pennymoor
Tiverton
Devon
EX16 8NB
Website: www.ukalpaca.com
Email: info@ukalpaca.com
Tel: 01884 841442

ARAGON YARNS
Online and onsite shop selling pure English wool from Romney
sheep. A really gorgeous yarn in a range of rich colours.
Aragon Farm
Sissinghurst
Cranbrook
Kent
TN17 2AB
Website: www.aragonyarns.co.uk
Tel: 01580 714400

CUCUMBERPATCH
97 High Street
Wolstanton
Newcastle-under-Lyme
Staffordshire
ST5 0EP
Website: www.cucumberpatch.co.uk
Email: sales@cucumberpatch.co.uk
Tel: 01782 862332

LOOP
Inspiring North London shop. Knitting classes and online store.
41 Cross Street, London
N1 2BB
Website: www.loopknitting.com
Tel: 020 7288 1160

PRICK YOUR FINGER
Shop, classes and gallery run by the girls from Cast Off.
260 Globe Road
Bethnal Green
London
E2 0JD
Website: www.prickyourfinger.com
Tel: 020 8981 2560

ECO, FAIRTRADE AND RECYCLED YARNS

MORAL FIBRE
Ethical importers of Fairtrade, eco-friendly and recycled yarns.
Stockists of MANGO MOON yarns from Nepal.
Moral Fibre House
B7 Tenterfield Business Park
Burnley Road
Luddenddenfoot
Halifax
West Yorkshire
HX6 2EQ
Website: www.moral-fibre.com
Email: sales@moral-fibre.com
Tel: 01422 886250

ROWAN YARNS
Contact details as above.
PURELIFE organic wool and cotton yarns coloured with natural dyes and British Breeds range.
REVIVE – a mix of recycled silk, cotton and viscose.

TWILLEYS OF STAMFORD
Contact details as above.
SINCERE organic cotton.

SIRDAR
Contact details as above.
SUBLIME organic wool and cotton.

Appendix: Guidance, hints and tips

The basics

Being a beginner is always frustrating. You see the possibilities and want to progress as quickly as possible. A short time spent learning how to hold the needles and the wool at this stage will make you a much more efficient knitter for life.

It may seem uncomfortable at first, but if you hold the needles and the wool properly your knitting will develop a rhythm and grow much faster. Once you have a confident rhythm going you will be able to relax and take your eye off the ball. Watch television, chat to friends, look at the scenery from a train or car window and all the while your knitting will be growing. One of the nicest things about knitting is that it is so portable and you can do other things at the same time.

Knitting know-how starts with a ball of wool and a pair of needles. I suggest you use short length size 5 mm needles and a ball of double knitting wool, as both are sturdy enough to be held comfortably and get swift results.

HOLDING THE YARN

Looping the yarn around the fingers of your right hand creates a controlled tension for feeding the wool through to the needles as you knit. Mastering this will help you to produce neat, even-tensioned knitting.

Weave the wool around your little finger (the pinkie) then under your ring and middle fingers and over your index finger. Use your pinkie to feed and adjust the tension of the wool. Practise so that this comes naturally and your knitting will be faster, more even and more rhythmic because of it.

These instructions are for right-handed knitters. If you are left-handed, I suggest you use a mirror to reflect the diagrams in reverse, but this doesn't work for everyone.

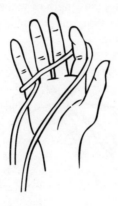

Figure A1 Holding the yarn.

Insight

> Try sitting directly opposite a right-hander and copying them – it will be like a mirror image and you'll be able to ask questions. On your own? Look at the left-handed knitting demonstrations on YouTube.com.

HOLDING THE NEEDLES

The English method
The English method is used to demonstrate the stitches in this book.

Hold the needle with the cast-on stitches in the palm of your left hand with your thumb across the stitches.

Keep the stitches 10–15 cm from the needle point: too near the point you risk losing them; too far away you will need to stretch the yarn as you knit.

Wind the yarn around the fingers of your right hand, as shown in Figure A1.

Hold the right needle between your thumb and index finger so that the needle lies on top of your hand following the line of your forearm.

Aim to knit with a taut 5 cm length of wool between your needles and your index finger so that you minimize the movements you have to make as you knit.

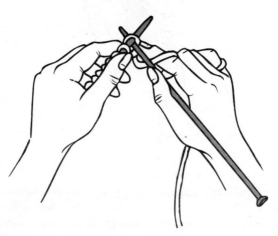

Figure A2 Holding the needles – the English way.

The Continental method
This seems to suit those who have learned to crochet before they learned to knit, and experts find it much faster. It also minimizes the movements you make when knitting.

Hold the needles with the cast-on stitches in your left hand.

Wind the yarn around the fingers of your left hand and twice around the index finger, keeping the ball of wool on the left.

The left hand is held still with the yarn tension created between the knitting, the index finger and the pinkie. The right hand holds the needle horizontally from above. The right needle is inserted through the stitch loop to draw the taut yarn through and make the new stitch while the knitted stitch is slipped off the needle. The new stitch remains on the right and further stitches are knitted until all the knitting is in the right hand.

The following row is started on the left once again.

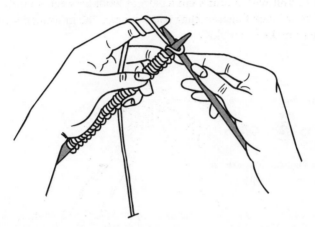

Figure A3 Holding the needles – the Continental way.

Insight

If you really can't hold the needles the 'right way', it's better to find your own style and get on with making things! I once knew a self-taught accordion player who only discovered after 10 years of great music making that he was playing his instrument upside down. So, if it works for you...

MAKING THE FIRST STITCH

The first stitch on the needle is a slipknot.

Twist the yarn around your finger and pull a loop through and place it on the needle.

Pull the short end of the wool to tighten the knot so that it sits neatly on the needle.

It should be tight enough to slide easily along the needle but not so loose as to drop off the end.

Figure A4 *Making the first stitch.*

CASTING ON

The two-needle method
Look at Figure A5.

1 *Hold the needle with the first slipknot stitch in your left hand. Hold the right-hand needle as if you were holding a pen, with the wool feeding over between the knuckles of your right hand. Insert the right needle through the stitch on the left.*
2 *Wrap the yarn under the right needle.*
3 *Slide the needle back drawing the yarn through the stitch.*
4 *Now place this new stitch on the left needle above the first stitch.*

You have now knitted your first cast-on stitch and can repeat this procedure to make as many stitches as you need.

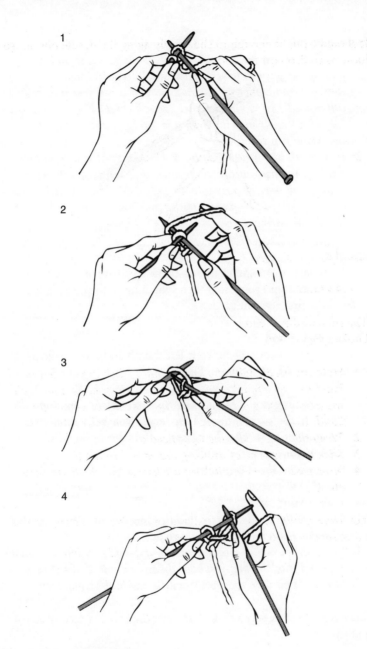

1

2

3

4

Figure A5 Casting on with two needles.

Casting-on tips

1 *Check that you keep the same tension as you cast on by pulling the yarn to firm up each stitch. Not too tight, though – remember you want a snug fit when you slide the other needle in to knit another cast-on stitch. If you have to force the needle into the loop it is too tight and if it drops out easily it is too loose.*

2 *It is worth being ruthless about the quality of your casting on. If your cast-on row looks uneven or too loopy then start again. You may be desperate to get on with your knitting, but a bad edge can't be fixed later on and could spoil the look of the whole garment.*

Insight

If your casting on comes up too tight, try using needles a size larger than those suggested then switching to the correct size from the first row onwards.

The thumb method

Stitches can be cast on using your left thumb and one needle held in the right hand, as shown in Figure A6.

1 *The first slipknot stitch is made approximately 1 m along the length of the yarn, although the length you need depends on the number of stitches being cast on. As a rough guide, use 1 m for every 100 stitches.*

2 *Holding the short end of the yarn in your left hand, wrap it round your thumb and keep its tension using your fingers against your palm.*

3 *Knit into the loop on your thumb using the yarn from the ball to make a stitch on the right needle.*

4 *Now make another loop on your thumb and knit into it to make a second stitch. When you have the right number of stitches, turn and knit with the yarn from the ball in the usual way.*

An edge made this way will be hard wearing, with a nice stretchy quality.

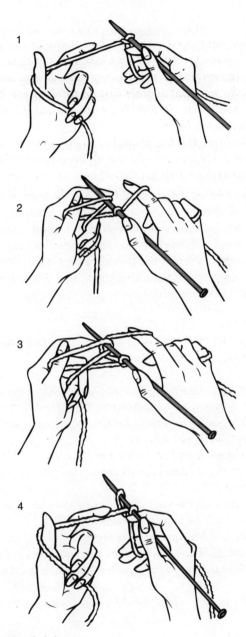

Figure A6 The thumb method of casting on.

There are several other variations in casting on and they produce different edges. If the stitches are made by knitting into the front of the stitch you create a looser edge, whereas knitting into the back makes the edge firmer. Stitches can also be made by inserting the right needle not into a stitch but into the space between two stitches.

Experiment to see which method suits you best.

Casting on with four needles
When you knit in the round using four double-pointed needles, the stitches are divided equally across three of them and the fourth is the working needle. In some countries, it is more common to knit in the round with five needles. This method is only suitable for knitting tubes, where it has two advantages: that there are no seams to be sewn and, for stocking stitch, that you only need to work in knit stitch, not purl. Fairisle patterns with lots of colour changes are done this way.

Cast on using your usual method. There are two ways to divide the stitches:

1 *Cast all the stitches onto one long needle, then slip them onto three double-pointed needles.*
2 *Cast on the first third, then introduce another needle next to it and cast on the next third, and do the same again for the final third.*

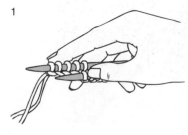 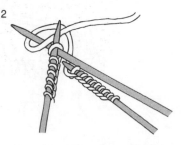

Figure A7 Casting on with four needles.

PICKING UP A DROPPED STITCH

This is bound to happen in the early stages, so now is a good time to learn how to correct it.

The easiest way to do this is to use a crochet hook as it will catch the loop of the stitch and hold onto it as you weave the dropped stitch back up through the bars until it reaches the row you are working on.

A knit stitch appears at the front of the bar and a purl stitch behind it.

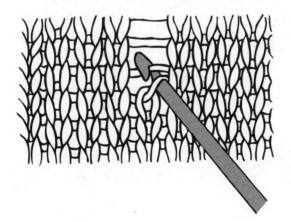

Figure A8 Picking up a dropped stitch – plain side.

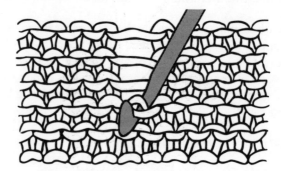

Figure A9 Picking up a dropped stitch – purl side.

UNPICKING MISTAKES

If you spot a mistake earlier in the row or the previous row do not despair. You need to work in reverse and 'unknit' to the point of your mistake.

Hold the work in your right hand and insert the left needle into the row below. Transfer this stitch back onto the left needle and allow the top stitch to drop off. Keep doing this until you reach the mistake, rework it, then continue knitting.

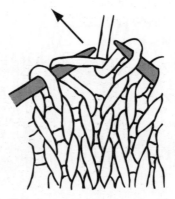

Figure A10 Unpicking – plain side.

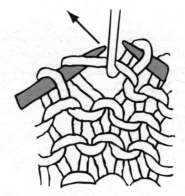

Figure A11 Unpicking – purl side.

INCREASING

When knitting any shape other than a square or rectangle it is
necessary to increase or decrease the number of stitches on the
needle. If the stitches are increased or decreased on the outside
edges it is called shaping, and when it is done within the row it is
known as fashioning. There are several different ways to do this
and each one gives a different visible decorative effect.

Increasing on the outside edge

The most basic shaping is done by casting on the required number
of stitches by the two-needle method at the beginning and end of
the row.

Figure A12 Increasing on the outside edge.

Increasing on the inside edge

This is done within the row. Knit into the stitch in the usual way, but before it is slipped off the left-hand needle bring the yarn forward and work a purl stitch into the same loop. This makes one extra stitch.

To create a symmetrical width increase, use this method on the third stitch from the beginning of the row and then again on the third stitch from the end of the row.

Figure A13 Increasing on the inside edge.

Pick-up increase (also called Make One)

This is done by picking up and knitting into the horizontal bar between the stitches from the previous row. The row is then continued in the usual way.

To create a symmetrical width increase, pick up and knit into the bar after the second stitch from the start of the row and the bar before the second stitch from the end of the row.

Increase using 'overs'

This is the most obviously decorative method of increasing within the row.

Do this by wrapping the wool over the needle to create a new loop, which is worked as a stitch in the following row.

Symmetrical width increases by this method are done by forming the new loop after the third stitch has been worked at the start of the row and then doing the same before the third stitch from the end of the row. Using an 'over' creates a neat hole, and a row of them will create an openwork pattern.

Double increases using 'overs'
These are done in the same way, by wrapping the yarn over the needle and knitting it as a stitch in the following row, except they are worked in pairs on each side of a central stitch within the row. They are most usually used to create pleats.

DECREASING

This reduces the number of stitches on the needle to make the work narrower. The simplest way to decrease is to knit two stitches together. The other method uses slipped stitches and is used for more decorative pattern work.

To give gradual shaping the decreasing is done on alternate rows and always on the plain row of stocking stitch.

When more than three stitches are to be decreased in succession, they are simply cast off at the start of the row.

Decreasing on the outside edge
Simple decreasing at the start of the outside edge is done by slipping the first stitch then knitting the second and passing the slipped stitch over it.

To decrease more than one stitch, slip the first, knit the next two or three together then pass the slipped stitch over.

If the edge is to be sewn up as a seam then the last two stitches in the row can simply be knitted together.

If a neater edge is required, use this method instead: at the end of the row, do not work the last stitch but slip it onto the right-hand needle, turn the work and begin the next row by working the slipped stitch, slipping the next one, then passing the first stitch over it.

Figure A14 Decreasing on the outside edge.

Single decreases within the row
Stitches decreased within the row and done by the slipped-stitch method create a decorative slanted pattern effect.

It is described in knitting patterns as sl1 k1 psso (slip one, knit one, pass slipped stitch over).

Symmetrical decreases
The decrease is worked in the purl row as sl1 p1 psso (slip one, purl one, pass slipped stitch over).

In a knit row the decrease forms a slant to the left on the front of the knitting, and on a purl row it forms a slant to the right on the front of the knitting.

Decreasing on the inside edge
When a sharper angle is required, more stitches are decreased at the ends of the rows.

To make a left-sloping decrease
Slip one, knit two together, pass slipped stitch over (sl1 k2tog psso).

To make a right-sloping decrease

Slip one knit-wise, knit the second, then pass the slipped stitch over it. Then move the stitch back to the left needle and pass the next left stitch over it before moving it onto the right needle.

Be assured that these initially perplexing instructions will soon become familiar as they form the basis of all shaping and most decorative openwork patterns in knitting.

Figure A15 Decreasing on the inside edge.

CASTING OFF

Casting off is the secure way to finish a piece of knitting and prevent your work from unravelling. There are several different ways to do this, some more suited to one stitch than another. As a rule of thumb, casting off should always be done in the pattern you are using – this is especially important where a rib stitch is being worked as a border. Work the casting off following the same knit and purl sequence as your pattern and the cast-off will keep the rib's stretchy quality. A plain knit cast-off row forms a fairly rigid chain that will restrict a garment's elasticity. It is important to relax your tension slightly when you cast off, as a tight edge will spoil the shape of your knitting.

Casting off 1

This is the most common way to cast off stitches. If you are working in rib, remember to keep knitting the plain and purl stitches for the cast-off row. See the diagram below.

1   *Work the first two stitches as usual, then use the point of the left needle to lift the first stitch over the second and off the end of the needle.*
2   *Now, knit one more stitch and do the same again, working just one stitch each time until a single stitch remains.*

Break the yarn and thread the end through this stitch and pull up firmly to secure it. The cast-off row will resemble a chain.

You can do this using a knit or purl stitch.

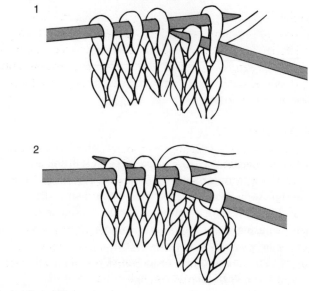

Figure A16 Casting off 1.

Casting off 2
This method makes a raised edge that has good elasticity.

It is especially useful for edges that are to be stitched together as seams.

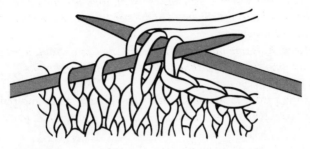

Figure A17 Casting off 2.

Knit two together (k2tog) through the back of the stitches. You will now have one stitch on the right needle. Slip it back onto the left needle and k2tog with the next stitch, into the back of the stitches as before. Continue in this way until just one stitch remains, then break the yarn, thread the end through the loop and pull it up firmly.

Crochet casting off
A crochet hook of the same gauge as the needles is used to cast off in a chain stitch, which gives a neat, firm and decorative edge to the work. It can be worked in a contrasting colour to finish off a hat or a blanket.

1 *Begin by using the crochet hook as you would the right knitting needle and knit the first two stitches from the left needle.*
2 *Now, use the crochet hook in its conventional way to draw the yarn through those two stitches.*
3 *You now have one new stitch on the crochet hook.*
4 *Knit the next stitch from the left needle onto the hook and once again draw the yarn through the two stitches.*
5 *Repeat this procedure until one stitch remains, then break the yarn, thread it though the loop and pull it up firmly.*

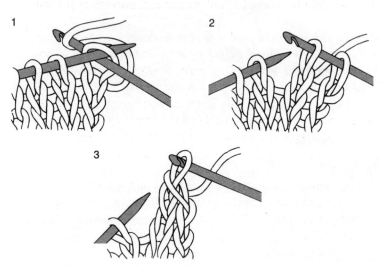

Figure A18 Crochet cast-off.

KNITTING WITH CIRCULAR NEEDLES

Circular needles are actually short rigid plastic or metal needles joined together with a length of bendable plastic. The needles come in a range of five length sizes, from 40 cm to 100 cm, and in the usual range of needle width sizes.

They can be used for conventional knitting or to knit garments in the round. Their only limitation is that when knitting in the round the garment has to have a 30 cm or wider circumference; anything smaller will need to stretch to meet up and will be better suited to knitting on a set of four needles. Examples of this would be gloves, children's socks and baby leggings.

To knit a tube, cast on the required number of stitches. Hold the needle with the last cast-on stitch on the right and join the circle by knitting into the first cast-off stitch on the left needle. Keep the yarn taut, as shown in Figure A19, as you bridge the gap and the join will not be obvious. All rounds are worked as knit but appear as stocking stitch on the outside of the tube. To knit garter stitch all rows must be worked as knit one round, purl the next round.

Circular needles can be used in the conventional way, as shown in Figure A20 (knitting then turning at the end of the row). When knitting very wide garments such as bedspreads, the plastic wire can hold about four times the number of stitches that a rigid needle would. It also allows the weight of the knitting to rest in your lap instead of being supported on the needles. This is something you will only really appreciate when you take on a large project, such as a throw.

Insight

The cast-on row always twists around on the needles. Check and untwist before you knit the first stitch – after that you're safe!

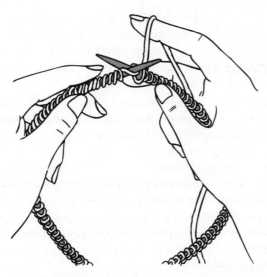

Figure A19 Using circular needles to knit in the round.

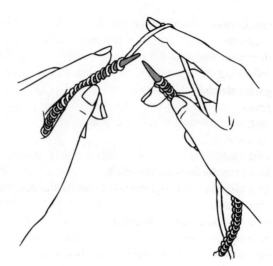

Figure A20 Using circular needles for conventional knitting.

Knitting abbreviations

If you are unfamiliar with knitting abbreviations, they can be extremely off putting. Patterns can resemble complex mathematical equations at a first and even a second glance. Abbreviations were introduced to compress long patterns but in doing so it seemed a whole new language had to be invented.

I hope that this book will help give you the confidence to unravel the mystery and to understand knitting patterns.

The important thing to remember is that all knitting is basically plain and purl with stitches added or taken away at regular intervals to produce the textured patterns:

**	the section between asterisks is to be repeated
alt	alternate
approx	approximate
beg	beginning
cc	contrasting colour

cm	centimetre
cont	continue
dec	decrease
foll	following
g st	garter stitch
g	gram
in	inch
inc	increase
k	knit
kb	knit into the back of the stitch
k1 b	knit into the centre of the stitch below the next one on the needle.
k2tog	knit two together to decrease
k up	pick up and knit
k-wise	knit-wise – as you would make a knit stitch
LH	left hand
m1	make one – increase by knitting into both front and back of next stitch
m1p	make one purl-wise
mc	main colour
mm	millimetre
ms	moss stitch
No	number
patt	pattern
psso	pass slipped stitch over
p	purl
p up	pick up and purl
p-wise	purl-wise – as you would make a purl stitch
rem	remaining
rep	repeat
rnd	round
RH	right hand
Rs	right side facing
sl	slip
sl st	slip a stitch without knitting it
st st	stocking stitch
tbl	through the back of the loop
tog	together
Ws	wrong side facing

It may take a bit of time to fathom the following yrns and yfwds but they are the ones used to make neat holes for lacework or eyelets:

ybk   yarn back between needles to the knit position
yfwd   yarn forward between needles to the purl position
yo/yon yarn wraps over the needle once from knit position – used between knit stitches
yrn   yarn round needle from purl position – used between purl stitches

CABLE ABBREVIATIONS

The number of stitches will vary according to the pattern:

cN   cable needle
c4B   slip 4 stitches onto a cable needle and keep them at the back
c4F   slip 4 stitches onto a cable needle and keep them at the front

---

How to knit various stitches

KNIT STITCH

Also called plain stitch.

Hold the needle with the cast-on stitches in your left hand.
Now look at Figure A21.

1 *Insert the tip of the right needle through the first stitch from front to back. Take the yarn round the back and under the right needle then over between the needles. Raise your right index finger to keep the yarn's tension as you do this.*
2 *Retract the right needle, helping it with a little push from the tip of your left index finger. Dip the right needle under the stitch, taking the loop of yarn with it. Slide the original stitch to the tip and drop it off the left needle.*
3 *You have knitted your first knit stitch!*

Continue to the end of the row then turn the work, swap hands and do the same again.

Now cast on 10 stitches and knit 10 rows.

Cast off.

This is your first piece of knitting and is worth saving.

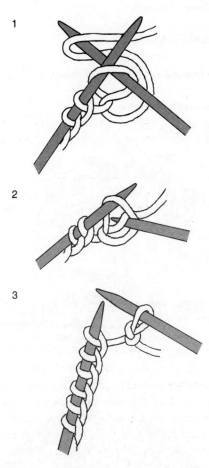

Figure A21 Knit stitch.

PURL STITCH

Follow Figure A22.

1 *Hold the needle with the cast-on stitches in your left hand and hold the yarn at the front of the right needle. Slide the tip of the right needle from right to left into the first stitch, with the right needle in front of the left. Pass the yarn round the needle point.*
2 *Draw the loop through.*
3 *Keep the stitch on the right needle and allow the original stitch to drop off the left needle.*

You have now knitted your first purl stitch.

Continue to the end of the row.

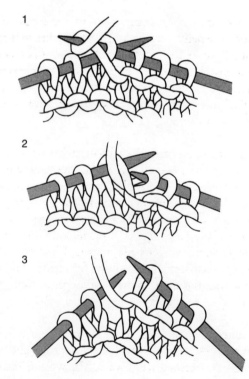

Figure A22 Purl stitch.

TWISTED GARTER STITCH

Twisted garter stitch is done by inserting the needle into the back of the stitch instead of the front. It has the same appearance as the usual garter stitch method (see page 19) but the texture is much firmer.

TWISTED STOCKING STITCH

A twisted stitch is made by inserting the needle into the back of the stitch instead of the front. Doing this on the knit row of stocking stitch (see pages 25–26) and working the purl row in the usual way produces a different, denser texture with a vertical zigzag effect. For a very minor variation, it creates a surprisingly noticeable difference.

RIB STITCHES

Ribbing is worked by alternating sets of knit and purl stitches. This gives the work elasticity, and 20 single rib stitches will appear half the width of 20 worked in stocking stitch. The rib can be stretched width-wise to match the stocking stitch, but it will spring back on release. Traditionally, jumpers have a ribbed neck opening, cuffs and welt, which is a term used to describe the band at the lower edge on the waist or hip.

There are also plenty of distinctive ribbing styles that are used as whole garment patterns in their own right. The single rib is explained below and the double rib on pages 29–30. The same method can be applied to knitting a triple or quadruple rib, by increasing the number of stitches in each set. The English or fisherman's rib is very popular for its warm insulating quality, and a single or double rib gives a snug body-hugging fit to skinny-rib jumpers. Children prefer ribbed jumpers because their stretchiness allows for plenty of movement and they can grow with the child, so they last longer as well.

Single rib
This is the simplest rib stitch and has the appearance of vertical lines of knit stitches. The purl stitches are set back and revealed when the work is stretched widthways. The work is identical on both sides.

Single rib can be worked on an odd or even number of stitches in straight knitting but only on an even number in circular knitting, where the same stitches are knitted and purled for every round.

It is done by working a knit and purl stitch alternately to the end of the row.

On the following row, the order reverses so you work a purl stitch first.

For an odd number of stitches:
Row 1: k1 p1.
Row 2: p1 k1.

For an even number of stitches:
Row 1: k1 p1 to end.
Row 2: k1 p1 to end.

Reversed rib
This pattern forms broad vertical stripes of raised plain stitches with an equal width of reversed stocking stitch in between. It does not have the elasticity of the previous two ribs, because each alternate row is worked as straight purl.

This rib is not suitable as an edging pattern.

Cast on in multiples of six.

Row 1: k3 p3.
Row 2: p.

Figure A23 Reversed rib.

Fisherman's rib

A new variation known as 'knitting below', abbreviated as k1b, is added for this rib stitch. To do this, the right needle is inserted into the middle of the stitch below the next one to be knitted. Knit it, then allow both 'stitches' to drop off the needle in the usual way. This is only done on a knit stitch – the purl is worked in the normal way.

Fisherman's rib creates a very warm, lightweight and stretchy fabric, much beloved by action-loving outdoorsy types who need maximum freedom of movement while keeping the elements at bay.

Cast on an even number of stitches.

Row 1: knit.
Row 2: k1*k1b p1* to last two stitches k1b k1.

These two rows form the pattern.

Figure A24 Fisherman's rib.

Wide rib

For this rib, an uneven number of stitches is worked in each set, giving a panelled effect of narrow lines running through the work.

Cast on in multiples of seven.

Row 1: k5 p2. Repeat to the end of the row.
Row 2: k2 p5. Repeat to the end of the row.

(Purl stitches knitted in the previous row and knit stitches previously purled.)

Twisted rib
This is a dense and attractive variation on the simple rib pattern. It has plenty of stretch and gives a slight herringbone effect.

To make a twisted stitch, the right needle is inserted into the back instead of the front of the next stitch on the left needle.

For an odd number of stitches:
Row 1: k1 p1 working into the back of the stitch.
Row 2: p1 k1 working into the back of the stitch.

For an even number of stitches:
Row 1: k1 p1 working into back of stitch.
Row 2: k1 p1 working into back of stitch.

Figure A25 Twisted rib.

MOSS STITCHES

Knitters very often declare moss stitch to be their absolute favourite (see page 39 for instructions for ordinary moss stitch). It is neat and unpretentious, doesn't curl at the edges and has a firm pebbled texture.

It is an ideal stitch for borders on blankets, edgings where buttons are used and for collars. There are plenty of variations but, at its most basic, it is worked on an odd number of stitches as k1 p1 on every row. The knit and purl stitches alternate rather than running in rows as they do with a single rib.

Double moss stitch
This variation is worked over four rows to produce a small diamond pattern.

Cast on an odd number of stitches.

Row 1: k1 *p1 k1* to the end.
Row 2: p1 *k1 p1* to the end.
Row 3: p1 *k1 p1* to the end.
Row 4: k1 *p1 k1* to the end.

Repeat these four rows.

Figure A26 Double moss stitch.

Insight
If you practise stitches by knitting squares, use the same weight of yarn and size of needles and you will be able to sew them together as a sampler.

TEXTURED PATTERNS

Trinity or blackberry stitch

This pattern has two names. The trinity refers to the method of knitting three stitches into one and then one stitch into three. The second name is more picturesque as the small bobbles resemble a mass of blackberries.

The stitch is one of the traditional Aran patterns worked in panels alongside cables and reverse stocking stitch.

Cast on stitches in multiples of four plus one.

The pattern appears complicated, but take it one stage at a time and you will discover that it is actually quite simple.

The k1 p1 k1 into the same stitch means that you do not slip the stitch off the left needle when you knit it, but bring the yarn forward and purl into the same stitch, then take the yarn back and knit into it again. Then allow it to drop off the needle in the normal way.

Row 1: p to end (RS).
Row 2: k1 *p3tog (k1 p1 k1) all into the same stitch*. Repeat to first stitch, k1.
Row 3: p to end.
Row 4: *p3tog (k1 p1 k1) all into the same stitch*. Repeat to end.

Basketweave stitch

This is a very simple way to add texture to a piece of knitting. It is worked in blocks of four or more stitches, but there are no hard and fast rules.

Cast on in multiples of twice the block size.

These are four stitches wide.

Rows 1–4: k4 p4. Repeat to the end.
Rows 5–8: p4 k4. Repeat to the end.

Figure A27 Basketweave stitch.

Other attractive textured patterns are the Betty Martin stitch (page 73) and lace rib (pages 70–71).

CABLE STITCH

Cables are part of the long tradition of knitting fishermen's sweaters using patterns that echo the shapes of ropes and cables on the boats. They are usually knitted in stocking stitch alongside reverse stocking stitch or another textured background stitch that gives them prominence. The twisting patterns appear to demand experience and skill levels beyond the novice knitter, but that is a part of their appeal. It is what makes knitting your first cable such a memorable achievement. Work practice squares of these simple cable patterns in order to understand the method and gain confidence to choose to knit a pattern that features cables.

- ▶ *Cables are created within a row by placing a set number of stitches onto a short double-pointed cable needle.*
- ▶ *This needle is held at the back or front of the row being worked.*
- ▶ *The same set number of stitches are then knitted from the left needle.*
- ▶ *The stitches on the cable needle are knitted next.*
- ▶ *This creates the twist at the start of the cable by moving stitches from one position in the row to another.*

The length of the cable is decided by the number of rows knitted in stocking stitch between the twists.

> **Insight**
>
> Cable is not as difficult as it looks, and the only way to find that out is to try it yourself. I was so proud of my first twisted cable sample square that I stitched it onto a plain cardigan as a pocket.

When the stitches on the cable needle are kept at the front of the work the cable will twist the stitches from right to left. See Figure A28.

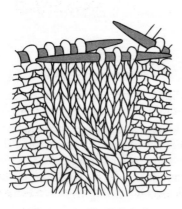 

Figure A28 Cable needle at front.

When the stitches on the cable needle are kept at the back of the work the cable will twist from left to right. See Figure A29.

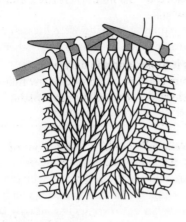

Figure A29 Cable needle at back.

Cables are often worked in oppositional pairs.

Small cable stitch
Cast on in multiples of five plus three.

Row 1: *p3 k2* to last three stitches p3.
Rows 2–4: stocking stitch.
Row 5: *p3 slip 1 onto cable needle and leave at the back of the work k1 then k1 from the cable needle* to last three stitches p3.

Repeat rows 2–5 as required.

Single cable stitch
Cast on in multiples of seven plus three.

Rows 1 and 3: *p3 k4* to last three stitches p3.
Rows 2, 4 and 6: *k3 p4* to last three stitches k3.
Row 5: *p3 slip 2 onto cable needle and leave at the back of the work k2 then k2 from the cable needle* to last three stitches p3.

Repeat as required.

OPENWORK STITCHES

There was a time when all the babies in the land were dressed in similar lacy knitted outfits lovingly made by their grandmothers. Fashions change and lacy patterns were dropped in favour of plainer, more linear styles. Now that retro and vintage have allowed the past back into our lives, an old-fashioned baby shawl or a lacy cashmere cardigan will be given the respect it deserves.

The stitches are more challenging because rows have to be counted, but not all lacework demands the same amount of concentration. The patterns described here are all easy to master and will add another dimension to your knitting. It is a fact that once you have been bitten by the knitting bug, your curiosity will eventually lead you to these more complex knitting patterns. If you avoid pastel colours, the patterns will have a different, more contemporary character.

Lace patterns are made with passed over slipped stitches and yarn over increases followed by decreases to make secure holes. Look at the abbreviations reminder to recap the terms used to describe these manoeuvres.

See also Turkish fagotting (pages 69–70) and mesh stitch (page 75).

Abbreviations reminder
k2tog	knit two together to decrease
psso	pass slipped stitch over
sl1	slip one stitch
yfwd	yarn forward between needles
yon	yarn over needle
m1	make one stitch

Cellular stitch
This is a plain open mesh stitch useful for babies' cotton blankets, string bags or beachwear. It features a single repeated pattern row that can be worked on any number of stitches. For best effect, knit this stitch on medium to large needles.

It has a tendency to stretch diagonally and will benefit from being blocked (see pages 140–141). If used for a baby blanket, a satin ribbon border will help keep the corners square.

Row 1: purl.
Row 2: k1 m1 (knit into the bar between the stitches) k1 pass the made stitch over the k1*.

Single eyelet pattern

This is a pretty stitch best worked in fine yarn. It is worked in multiples of eight and is particularly suited to baby clothes. It is not difficult but requires careful stitch counting until you have the pattern established and can refer to the previous eyelet positions. The k2tog on the first pattern row reduces the number of stitches on the needle and the m1 in the following row puts them back leaving a neat little hole.

Row 1: k.
Row 2: *p3 k2tog p3 repeat from *to end of the row.
Row 3: *k3 m1 (pick up and knit the bar between the stitches) k4 repeat from * to end of the row.
Row 4: p.
Row 5: k.
Row 6: p1 *p6 k2tog repeat from * to last 7 sts p7.
Row 7: k1 *k6 m1 k1 repeat from * to last 7 stitches k7.
Row 8: p.

Figure A30 Single eyelet pattern.

How to knit from a pattern

Knitting patterns are set out in a standard way. The key ingredients at the start of the pattern are sizing, yarn requirements, needle size, tension and abbreviations.

The pattern has been designed to fit an average size for an adult or an average aged child. This measurement will appear first in the pattern, followed by another **square-bracketed** series of numbers referring to gradual increases in size.

For example:

> **Child's sweater**
> **Age** 2 *[4: 6: 8: 10]*
> **To fit chest** 56 *cm [61: 66: 71: 76]*
> **Double knitting wool** *Number of balls required 6 [6: 7: 7: 8]*
> **Needles** *1 pair 4 mm, 1 pair 3.75 mm*
> **Tension** 22 *stitches and 28 rows per 10 cm square*
> **Abbreviations used** *alt = alternate; beg = beginning; cont = continue; k = knit; p = purl*

The pattern will then be set out in sections such as front, back, sleeves.

Asterisks show what section of the row is to be repeated.

For example:

> *Using 4 mm needles cast on 68 [74: 84: 90: 96] stitches.*
> *Row 1: k1 *p2 k2* to last stitch, k1.*

This means you are beginning and ending the row with a knit stitch but in between you are working a rib stitch.

Round brackets are used to show pattern instructions that are to be repeated, and the brackets will be followed by a number. For example:

> *(yfwd, sl1, k1 psso) x2*

This means: bring the yarn to the front, slip one stitch onto the right needle without knitting it, knit one stitch then use the left needle to lift the slipped stitch over the last knit stitch and then off the needle. The brackets and number denote that this sequence must be followed twice.

You can now see why abbreviations are necessary!

Alphabet chart

The chart in Figure A31 provides a basic A to Z for knitting initials.

Try experimenting on graph paper to design your own version.

How to measure

Pattern dimensions will be listed, but it is also a good idea to take the measurements of the lucky person you are knitting for – and that includes yourself.

Measure these key areas:

> **Chest:** *straight across the back under the arms and across the fullest part of the chest.*
> **Shoulder:** *from the tip of the shoulder to the base of the neck.*
> **Neck:** *around the neck at collar level.*
> **Armhole depth:** *from top of shoulder to 2.5 cm below the armhole.*
> **Underarm to waist:** *from 2.5 cm below armpit to natural waistline.*
> **Hip:** *around the fullest part of the hips.*
> **Arm:** *around the fullest part of the upper arm.*
> **Sleeve length:** *from 2.5 cm below armpit to the inside wrist.*
> **Wrist:** *around the arm just above the wrist bone.*

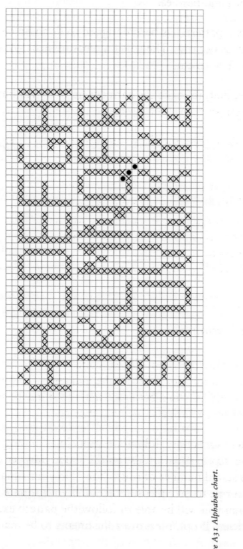

Figure A31 Alphabet chart.

If you need to make any adjustments, you can refer to the tension. This tells you how many stitches there will be per 10 cm and how many rows are worked to give a depth of 10 cm when using the suggested yarn and needles.

For example, a pattern has been designed to fit an 80 cm bust and has 120 stitches per row. The tension measurement gives a width of 20 stitches per 10 cm.

This tells you that, to make the garment fit an 85 cm bust, you will need to add another 10 stitches, so you cast on 130 stitches.

The same pattern gives the sleeve measurement as 44 cm. The tension measurement gives a depth of 28 rows per 10 cm.

This tells you that to shorten the sleeve length by 4 cm you would need to work 7 fewer rows than the pattern suggests. (**Note:** this will only be relevant if you are using a pattern such as cable or Aran, where certain numbers of rows make up the design. If the sleeves are shaped with increases or decreases then it is best to add or take off length in a straight section where these do not occur.)

The tension square

Most beginners are impatient to begin and it is difficult to persuade them to knit a 10 cm square before the main event. However, it is important – it makes you a better knitter and it makes sure you don't spend weeks knitting something that doesn't fit.

To make a tension square, follow the guidelines in the pattern for knitting a 10 cm square. Cast on the stated number of stitches and knit the stated number of rows. Now pin your square out flat and use a rule to take measurements. If your square measures 10 cm × 10 cm you will be able to follow the pattern exactly as it has been written. If not, there are adjustments to be made.

The width or horizontal tension is the most important one to get right as the length can be adjusted by knitting fewer or more rows.

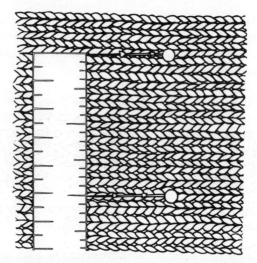

Figure A32 Counting stitches.

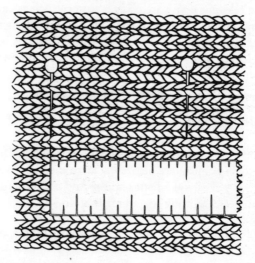

Figure A33 Counting rows.

CHANGING NEEDLE SIZE

The size of the needles used with the same yarn will change the size of the sample quite dramatically. The examples show three yarn weights knitted on fine 2 mm needles and again on large 6 mm needles.

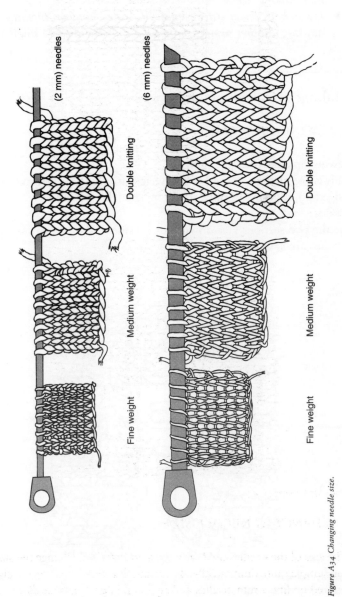

(2 mm) needles

Double knitting

Medium weight

Fine weight

(6 mm) needles

Double knitting

Medium weight

Fine weight

Figure A.34 Changing needle size.

- ▶ If your tension sample has more stitches than the stated number per 10 cm, try knitting another sample on needles that are one size larger.
- ▶ If you have fewer stitches than the stated number, then try knitting another sample on needles that are one size smaller.

Making up, blocking and pressing

SEWING UP SEAMS

Sewing up edge-to-edge seams
This is the method to use for lightweight garments as it forms no ridge and, if done carefully, it will be virtually invisible.

Lie the two sections face down, side by side so that the rows and stitches are aligned.

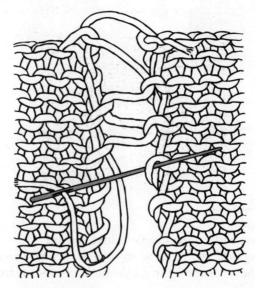

Figure A35 Sewing up edge-to-edge seams.

Thread a tapestry needle and, using a single strand of matching yarn, sew though loops of opposite stitches alternately.

Do not pull the yarn too tight as it will lose its elasticity.

Backstitching side seams
This method is better for chunkier garments, rib stitch and where you have added a special edge that is different from the main body of the garment pattern. This is most similar to the seams you make when working with fabrics.

Place the two pieces together with their right sides facing.

Align the rows and the stitches.

Thread the needle with a single strand of matching yarn and sew through the centre of adjacent stitches, taking the needle back to complete the stitch then a matching length forward to make a new stitch.

Keep the stitches the same size and do not pull the yarn too tight.

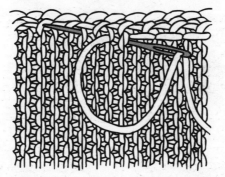

Figure A36 Backstitching seams.

Joining seams with a three-needle knitted cast-off
This is a very neat way to finish off shoulder seams. You need three needles of the same size – one for the back, one for the front and one to knit with.

Once the front and back sections have been completed, do not cast off. Instead, keep the stitches on the needle – a stitch holder can be used until you are ready to knit the edges together.

Place the back and front sections together with wrong sides facing each other.

Line up the needles holding the two sections in your left hand with the needle points facing the same way.

Use the spare needle in your right hand to knit through a stitch from both needles at the same time.

Cast off in the usual way until you have one stitch left on each needle, then break the yarn, thread through and pull to make a secure knot.

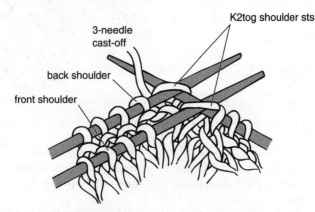

Figure A37 Joining seams with a knitted cast-off.

BLOCKING

Knitted garments all benefit from being given this treatment before they are sewn up. It does not take a great deal of time and it will make the assembling all the easier if every piece has been blocked.

Be sure to use stainless steel pins as other metals may leave rust marks:

▶ *Cover a tabletop with a thick towel or a blanket topped with a sheet.*
▶ *Place the pieces face down on the sheet.*
▶ *Check the measurements given for each piece in the pattern.*
▶ *Pin the pieces down to match those measurements, making sure that the rows run in straight lines.*
▶ *Rib should be stretched lightly widthways to open it out slightly.*

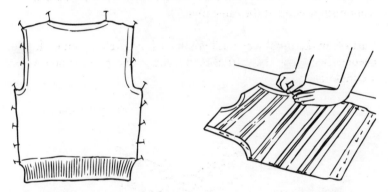

Figure A38 Blocking.

Insight

How tempting it is to race through the final stages and miss out the blocking! Of course you can, but if you want your garment to look its best, this stage will make all the difference.

PRESSING

After blocking, the garment is dampened and pressed to 'fix' the shape. This can be done by spraying with a mist of clean water and leaving it to dry naturally, but using a steam iron or a warm iron and a damp cloth is quicker and more effective.

▶ Place the damp cloth on the knitting and press the iron directly, but lightly, down onto it.
▶ Do not exert any real pressure as this will spoil the texture of the knitting.
▶ Do not move the iron as you do for normal ironing.
▶ Lift and press repeatedly until you have covered all the pieces.
▶ Do not remove any of the pins until the work is bone dry.

Figure A39 Pressing.

Index